Living
with
Urban
ildlife

John Bryant

Foreword by Pippa Greenwood
Illustrations by Barry Small

CENTAUR PRESS
London

First published in 2002 by Centaur Press
an imprint of Open Gate Press
51 Achilles Road, London NW6 1DZ

British Library Cataloguing-in-Publication Programme
A catalogue reference for this book is available from the
British Library.

ISBN: 0 900001 49 6

Produced by Bookchase (UK) Ltd
Printed and bound in Great Britain by Biddles Ltd. *www.biddles.co.uk*

John Bryant has been involved in the cause of animal protection for more than three decades. During that time he held several voluntary and professional positions including Vice Chairman of the RSPCA's national council, Chairman of the Council of Animal Aid, manager of the Ferne Animal Sanctuary and Chief Officer of the League Against Cruel Sports. Following his resignation from the League in September 1997, he spent a year as a consultant to the Campaign for the Protection of Hunted Animals and advisor to Member of Parliament, Michael Foster, in his attempt to pilot an anti-hunting Bill through the House of Commons. John is now an animal welfare consultant specialising in helping urban dwellers find humane solutions to problems with wildlife, particularly foxes. His previous book, *Animal Sanctuary*, is also published by Centaur Press.

Pippa Greenwood regularly appears on BBC radio and television in a variety of gardening and scientific programmes. She is gardening columnist for *The Mirror* newspaper and, in addition, regularly writes for *BBC Gardener's World* Magazine, *Amateur Gardening* and *Garden Answers*. Among her many best-selling books are *New Gardener, Garden Pests and Diseases* and *Pippa's Organic Kitchen Garden*. Her next book will be *A Garden for All Seasons*.

Author's note:

Names and addresses of suppliers of the various
repellents and deterrent devices mentioned in the
text may be found in Appendix 1.

Other useful addresses are listed in Appendix 2.

All products mentioned in this book should, of
course, be used with due care for both human
and animal safety, and strictly in accordance
with the manufacturer's instructions.

Contents

List of Illustrations

Foreword

I was born in London and spent many years there. I now
live in rural Hampshire. In both locations I have seen a
good range of wildlife, and been pleased to see it in both
its 'natural' and its more 'man-made' habitats. Whether it
is an urban fox or badger, or any other wild mammal or
bird, I still find spotting it gives me a thrill, but will admit
that on occasion, the local wildlife population can cause
irritation and distress, particularly to those who enjoy
gardening and especially those who aim to achieve a neat
and tidy look.

If you have found that wildlife is causing you problems,
you will not necessarily have felt that bringing about its
death is the solution. I hope not. In most cases, once the
creature has been killed, word gets out that there is a vacant
territory and in no time at all your garden will simply have

new replacement wildlife residents. So there is often little to be gained from your point of view, and a lot to be lost from that of the animals! Killing is something we should all avoid – and indeed most of us prefer to take the 'live and let live' approach – but I am always interested to hear about methods of persuading potentially damaging creatures away from certain areas of my garden.

By allowing wildlife to visit your garden you can add a new, positive dimension to gardening and at the same time provide a much-needed habitat. It is not a one-sided relationship, and I always feel that it is worth remembering that the wildlife, or at least its ancestors, was generally there before us. Wildlife has learned to put up with us, so surely we should reciprocate.

At last there is an easy-to-read and fascinating book to help you make the right choices about urban wildlife, written by a man who really knows his stuff. He not only understands and explains clearly the life cycles and habits of many types of wildlife, but also has tremendous practical experience when it comes to persuading it to change those habits, or perhaps even to move elsewhere. *Living With Urban Wildlife* is a book you will use time and time again.

Pippa Greenwood

Introduction

The last few decades of the twentieth century made us all more conscious of the incredible impact our highly successful species has had on the world. We have learned that our seemingly unstoppable, headlong industrialisation and intensification of farming involved such huge levels of destruction of habitats and pollution of the planet's delicate fabric that countless species of animals, birds and plants have been driven to the brink of extinction and beyond.

Many of us have a conscience about the rampage of our species around the planet. Consciousness awakens concern – hence the burgeoning of conservation and wildlife protection bodies and the competition amongst political parties for the 'green' vote. We have also become more tolerant of the many wild creatures that share our immediate environment. We are more inclined to use less- or non-toxic chemicals in our gardens and many people actively encourage wildlife by creating ponds, planting wild flowers and adding other wildlife-friendly features.

However, there is no doubt that some wild animals and birds can be a real nuisance, capable of creating unsightly or expensive damage to gardens, bowling greens, sports fields and golf courses. Foxes, badgers, squirrels and moles can damage lawns, greens and fields. Fox cubs can uproot or crush plants, dig holes in flower beds and defecate on lawns, patios and garden furniture. Squirrels can damage plants, dig up bulbs, raid bird tables and, if they gain access to lofts, strip electrical insulation and gnaw through roof timbers. Pigeons and other birds can create mess and damage buildings and of course rodents can cause damage and foul foodstuff.

Many old-fashioned ways of dealing with such 'pests', such as trapping, poisoning, and shooting are often in-effective as well as being expensive, dangerous and involving levels of cruelty that are unacceptable to most people today. Many such methods have either been out-lawed or require licences. The Wildlife & Countryside Act 1981, Wild Mammals (Protection) Act 1996, Protec-tion of Animals Act 1911 (1912 in Scotland), Protection of Badgers Act 1992, Pests Act 1954, Abandonment of Animals Act 1960, Animal By-Products Order 1999,

Agriculture Act 1999, Control of Pesticides Regulations 1986 and the Food & Environment Protection Act 1985, are only some of the laws with which modern 'pest' controllers need to be familiar if they are to avoid prosecution.

Fortunately both modern technology and our knowledge of biology are now sufficiently advanced to enable the successful resolution of most wildlife nuisances safely, inexpensively, effectively and legally – without causing harm to the culprits. And that is what this book is all about. It aims to assist individuals and families who find wild animals or birds causing them a genuine problem, but who wish to resolve matters without causing either pain or death to the culprits. The methodology is simple and works on the principle of making the problem area less attractive and less comfortable for the wild creatures which are causing the problem.

As readers may have noticed already, on the rare occasions the word 'pest' appears in this book, it is always in inverted commas. This is because I refuse to label any species of living creature as a 'pest' – any more than any plant species should be stereotyped as a 'weed'. It all depends on where it is and what it is doing. A herd of elephants wandering in the African savannah could not be fairly described as 'pests', but if you awoke one morning to find they had spent the night in your garden you could be forgiven for using the 'p' word – and much worse!

Mammals

Foxes

British population of breeding-age adults: 240,000

Calendar

January – Mating.

March – Cubs born (53-day gestation).

April/May – Cubs appear above ground.

August/October – Dispersal of cubs.

October/November – Establishment of territories.

December – Vixens establishing dens (earths).

The red fox is arguably both Britain's most beautiful and controversial mammal. Highly adaptable with an extremely catholic diet, foxes can thrive both in the UK's sparsest upland areas and in our busiest cities. However, although at the onset of winter there are around a quarter of million adult foxes in Britain, their life expectancy is less than a fifth of the 10–12-year life-span they should enjoy.

In the countryside fox hunting with hounds, terriers, lurchers, guns, snares (and illegal traps and poisons) means that it is an uncommon fox that survives until its second birthday. In the towns and cities, intentional persecution is much less of a problem (this is why urban foxes are so bold), but that most lethal of all predators, the motor car, leaves the town fox with no better life expectancy than its country cousin.

In early spring when the cubs are born, the fox population rises briefly to around two-thirds of a million individuals and yet by the next breeding season the population has returned to a quarter of a million. This means that every year 400,000 foxes die – as in all wild-life populations, mostly the very young. At least half of this huge death rate is due to man, either deliberate or accidental. Some might ask, 'What would happen if we stopped killing foxes? Wouldn't we be knee-deep in them very quickly?' The answer is no. The population has to equate with the available food. When fox numbers begin to rise to a level that cannot be sustained, one of two (or both) things happen. Fewer vixens produce cubs, or those that do have smaller litters. The average fox-cub litter in the UK is 4.5, but this can be less or more, dependent on the availability of a fox-friendly environment.

B.SMALL

The same is true of all wild animals and birds, and is easily demonstrated by, for instance, birds of prey. In Britain, all birds of prey such as eagles, buzzards, sparrow hawks, falcons, kestrels and owls are protected by law. Except for a few gamekeepers breaking the law, no one kills birds of prey, so why isn't the sky black with them? The answer is that there is not enough food and not enough territories to sustain flocks of eagles!

The massive mortality of foxes makes virtually no impact on the overall fox population density, but does result in a very young population. I once came across a very happy and contented 16-year-old domesticated fox, but in the wild, whether urban or rural, an 'old fox' is as rare as a happy 'pet' fox.

Fox populations are largely governed by the year-round availability of food and strong territorial defence. In the highlands of Scotland where natural food for foxes is sparse, a fox family's territory may consist of 40 square kilometres, whereas an urban fox family may find sufficient resources in a territory of only 40 acres. Whether in town or country, science has proved that killing foxes is pointless if the object is to reduce numbers. Removing foxes merely creates vacant territories for other foxes to occupy; there are always itinerant foxes looking for vacancies. The fox hunting fraternity hounds 20,000 foxes to death every year and the 'spade and terrier brigade' probably kill four times that number in their even nastier version of 'sport'. The fact that these people can hunt and kill foxes throughout the year (the only month of the year when there is no fox hunting with hounds is June) shows that this slaughter has nothing to do with 'pest' control.

Fox hunters make sure that they never run short of foxes in any particular part of their hunting 'country' by building cosy artificial earths and providing plenty of food in the form of dead sheep and chickens to create an artificially high fox population. In the nineteenth century and before, there was such a demand for foxes for hunting with hounds that thousands were imported from continental Europe and sold through London's Leadenhall Market where Hunt Masters queued to pay half-a-crown (12.5p) each for them. Others were supplied by gamekeepers who were no doubt delighted to receive a few shillings for animals they would otherwise destroy as 'vermin'.

Killing urban foxes in an effort to reduce their numbers or solve any problems caused by them is equally pointless. The Tonbridge-based Fox Project and its director Trevor Williams have been highly successful in promoting this logic to the local authorities of London, south-east England and beyond. Almost all these councils long ago abandoned the costly exercise of using 'pest control officers' to trap and kill problem foxes. These days, all but a few councils usually refer complaints about urban foxes to the Fox Project, or the National Fox Welfare Society or wildlife consultants such as myself, rather than spend council funds on expensive, unpopular and meaningless killing.

The Fox Project has perfected the art of using safe chemical deterrents to persuade problem foxes to stop digging, fouling, or causing other nuisance. Foxes, like dogs and to a lesser extent cats, rely on their noses to gauge and test their environment for food, competitors and danger. Chemical deterrents introduce strong confusing smells into the fox's environment and induce a level of anxiety and confusion which normally results in the fox avoiding the immediate area to one degree or another. Some deterrents can be used to mimic scent-marking by some unseen competitor species, or may merely persuade the fox to go somewhere where its nose is free of strange and annoying scents. The Fox Project provides an Advice Line on deterrence or can arrange for an experienced consultant to visit, investigate the problem and place various choices of deterrents in the best way to solve the problem.

The chemicals used are all approved products – the use of non-approved chemicals being the serious offence of misuse of pesticides which can lead to prosecution under the Food & Environment Protection Act. One of the best known deterrents for foxes, badgers, rabbits and moles is Renardine, which is a tar-like liquid similar in many ways to creosote, the wood preservative. However, creosote is highly toxic and not approved as an animal deterrent; its use as an alternative to Renardine would be misuse and therefore a criminal offence.

A keen gardener need only visit a good garden centre to find a vast armoury of safe chemicals for deterring nuisance animals (domestic or wild) from one's garden. They all work, although not every time and not in every situation. The time of the year in the animal's biological calendar needs to be taken into account, as does examination of the area of nuisance to determine the motivation of the animal concerned. Perhaps the first lesson to learn in trying to put an end to, or at least abate, a wildlife problem is that every fox, squirrel, rabbit, mole, mouse, pigeon, starling etc. is an individual. Half a litre of Renardine in one garden may result in a nuisance fox never being seen again. In an identical garden, another fox may seemingly ignore several litres of the same chemical. Similarly a chemical used to prevent animals fouling or digging up a lawn may work in the summer, but be totally ineffective in the winter after the first frosts.

Wild animals often use their urine and faeces to inform other animals, both of their own kind and other potential competitors, that the territory is occupied. Unlike domestic cats, which usually attempt to cover their faeces, foxes want everybody to see and smell theirs! I have seen lawns covered in very smelly fox faeces whereas in other gardens visited by foxes there may be none, or just the odd dropping or brown urine stain on the lawn. One fox family I encountered insisted on placing their nightly droppings on wrought iron garden furniture. Others foul on patios and doorsteps. Fox faeces, like those of other carnivores such as cats and dogs, can carry parasites such as roundworm or tapeworms; therefore if young children play on fouled lawns there is at least a theoretical risk that they could ingest such parasites from dirty fingers stuck in mouths or by eating food without firstly washing hands.

Much has been written about *Toxocara canis* 'roundworms' leading to blindness in children, but the risk of foxes being responsible for transmission of such diseases to children is much lower than transmission from domestic cats and dogs. According to the authoritative *Black's Veterinary Dictionary*, research has shown that two out of every hundred London residents have at sometime been infected by *Toxocara*. This is not surprising when one considers that one survey revealed that 24.4 per cent of soil samples from British public parks contained *Toxocara* eggs, although other surveys of parks and playing fields have given a lower average figure of 7 per cent for viable *Toxocara* eggs. Clearly the contribution by foxes to this appalling state of affairs is negligible, although it is fair to say that fox faeces is far from the most pleasant material to be found in a garden! Fortunately, the nuisance can usually be dramatically reduced and often prevented altogether.

A tried and tested product for treating lawns and plants upon which foxes (or cats and dogs) are fouling, is Scoot – available from garden centres. This is a powder containing aluminium ammonium sulphate, which is dissolved in water and sprayed onto the grass, beds or plants to be protected. It is also recommended that Scoot should be sprayed onto peas, seedbeds and seedlings to deter small rodents and birds. The product is virtually odourless to humans, but emits a disconcerting aroma to foxes and other animals. Experience shows that Scoot is not effective in frost, but then foxes rarely cause serious fouling and digging problems when the earth is hard and frosty

Get Off My Garden granules contain methyl nonyl ketone and smell strongly of citronella. The crystals can be lightly scattered on lawns, beds or in flower tubs to prevent fouling or digging. The granules can also be scattered on patios or paths, although personally I prefer to use Wash and Get Off spray on such hard surfaces. It is best to remove faeces with plastic 'poop-scoop' bags (available from supermarkets and pet shops) before treating the actual spot with the spray.

Two words of caution. Firstly *never allow any chemicals to enter ponds or anywhere else used as shelters by frogs, toads or any other amphibian.* Secondly, occasionally you may find that a fox tries to fight the smelly intruder and out-scent what it may think is a competitor. If so, merely pick up the faeces again and re-spray the spot. The chemical will win in the end!

Renardine is the most well-known repellent. It has been in use for more than 100 years and is approved as a deterrent for foxes, cats, dogs, rabbits, moles and badgers. Like all the chemicals mentioned here, the containers (one- and five-litre cans, and a spray) have full instructions either printed on the container or in enclosed leaflets. Renardine should not be applied to lawns and plants as it burns foliage. If your garden is being damaged or fouled by visiting foxes, or there is some other reason why you wish to deter foxes from your property, it is well worth spending some time carefully examining your entire garden for signs of fox movement and activity. The average urban fox family territory will include up to 100 average-size gardens and possibly a school, park or allotments. The foxes will patrol the territory regularly, or at least the parts containing life's necessities. In their minds will be a map containing every feature – ponds for a drink, compost heaps for succulent worms and the occasional nest of rodents, bird tables from which to scavenge scraps, freshly dug earth and the best lawns in which to find earth worms and cockchafer larvae, and the rabbit and guinea-pig hutches which somebody might just have forgotten to shut properly! As well as knowing personally every cat in the neighbour-hood and whether the cat is aggressive or tolerant of visitors, the local foxes will also know in which gardens they are likely to encounter a dog out for its last pee.

Most importantly, the foxes will visit those people who feed them (you can be sure there is at least one in every urban fox territory), and vixens will regularly check garden sheds to see where a little bit of digging will provide them with a future dry under-floor earth in which to produce cubs in early spring.

Careful examination of your garden could reveal many such signs. If you have wooden fencing, you may find that foxes have dug underneath for easy access to, and exit from, your garden. Look at the fence panels – you may find scratches and muddy patches where foxes leap over regularly. Thin vertical scratches are made by cats, but fox claws make thicker scratches that towards the top of the fence may be angled or even horizontal. This is because foxes sometimes 'roll' over the top of fences like human high jumpers. At the take-off and landing points the soil will be smooth from regular fox traffic and you may be able to see the footprints.

Look carefully at your lawn, particularly when the grass is quite long. You may be amazed that you can suddenly see a well-marked trail that you never noticed before. It may run from one fence to another (which is fine, because it means the fox is merely passing through and is not particularly attracted to your garden). Or the trail may run to your pond where the visiting foxes regularly stop by for a drink or to snatch the odd frog, or to your dustbin or your bird table or some other place a fox might think worth checking – just in case!

You might find a fox's lying-up place sheltered against the fence under dense shrubs, complete with the odd tennis ball, a shoe, a few bones and a dog's toy or two. Or you might find a freshly dug fox earth, so deep you can't reach the end of it with a long stick.

The Fox Project and I have found that the most effective method of using Renardine to deter foxes from gardens is by slightly diverting from the manufacturer's instructions, which recommend mixing the liquid with sand and sprinkling it evenly over the area to be protected. We prefer to use the liquid in a way that more closely replicates how a rival predator might scent-mark the territory. At the fox's access and exit points, and in any 'lying-up' places, place a small pile of sand, say 7–10 cm, high. Then, after *vigorously shaking* the can, pour some Renardine onto the pile.

If you find you have a fox earth in your garden, or under your shed, then you must proceed very carefully if you wish the foxes to move to one of the other dens that you can be sure they have in reserve elsewhere in their territory.

Firstly, from February to May you should assume the

earth is occupied by a vixen with cubs. Pour some Renardine onto two pieces of old rag, and with a stick carefully push the rag under the shed or, if the fox has dug a natural earth, into the entrance. In the latter case firmly push the rag into the soil down inside the tunnel so as to allow the animals to pass it without covering themselves in the substance. In the case of an earth under a shed, again try to place the rag so that the foxes can come out without getting it on their fur. You are only scent-marking the hole to give the resident the message that its den has been discovered and that it would be a good idea to find somewhere safer. Disturb the entrance all you like, and if you have a dog allow it to urinate there (and if no one is looking you could do the same!)

The next step is to place sticks (the small green garden canes are ideal) over the entrance, like a grill. Make sure they are pushed into the soil just firmly enough to prevent them being blown around by the wind, and place them around an inch apart covering the entire entrance, or entrances if there are more than one. Next day check whether the canes have been disturbed. If so replace them and check again the following day. You must ensure that the sticks remain undisturbed for at least forty-eight hours before you assume the den has been deserted and it is safe to fill it in or seal it off.

Chemical deterrents such as Renardine are usually highly effective in persuading adult foxes to avoid an area, but don't expect cubs to react in the same way. I have lost count of the number of people who have told me that they have soaked rags in Renardine and tied them on sticks and string all round their garden in an effort to prevent cubs from flattening their flower beds, only to look out to see the cubs playing with the rags. The fact is cubs are not old enough to know that one day scent will be their most important source of information and that strange new smells may well represent danger. In later paragraphs I mention other methods of deterring fox cubs.

Occasionally, foxes gain access to places where you cannot use pungent chemicals, such as under houses (usually through broken air-bricks) or under school Portakabin-type classrooms. The solution in such cases is to manufacture a one-way gate, which will allow foxes to emerge, but not allow them back in. A drawing of a such a gate is shown on the next page, but on no account should they be used until cubs have grown old enough to have been observed using the entrance – otherwise a fraught vixen might be excluded and prevented from getting back to her cubs. The cubs may not be experienced enough to find their way through the one-way gate and may perish from thirst and starvation while their frantic mother suffers great anguish and possibly terminal mastitis due to surplus milk.

When using a one-way gate at any time, a thin layer

of sand should be spread inside the entrance, and checked daily for footprints of any foxes still under the building. Once a few days have gone by with no disturbance of the sand, it will be safe to permanently seal the entrance.

perspex window

Electric fencing

Electric fencing and netting are commonly used in the countryside to keep livestock in and predators out, but this method of deterrence can also be useful in urban areas, particularly to protect vulnerable sports surfaces such as bowling greens and cricket wickets. Such barriers have proved to be highly effective against foxes as can be seen from the results of an experiment conducted in the mid-1970s at Forvie National Nature Reserve,

Aberdeenshire. Foxes had increasingly been preying on nesting sandwich terns, eider and mallard. Consequential desertion and abandonment of nesting areas were in fact having a more serious impact on bird numbers than actual predation, but the overall effect of fox incursion into the reserve threatened the very reason for the establishment of the reserve.

The erection of a simple three-wire electric fence across the reserve reduced activity within the reserve by 84 per cent. The wires were set 15 cm apart with the lowest 15 cm from the ground. A further wire at the foot of the fence acted as an earth. The wires were supported by Koltec nylon insulators on steel posts and the electric charge generated by Koltec Big Tom fencer units – one per 1000 metres of fence. The fencer unit was powered by a 10-volt battery, which normally lasts for 2 to 3 months of operation. Where foxes are attempting to dig under normal wooden or chain link fences, a single strand electric fence running along the foot of the fence, 15 cms from the ground and 15 cms out, will normally prevent foxes from digging and may even deter climbing, although a horizontal overhang at the top of the fence may be needed too.

There is also a specialist company, Electranets Ltd of Gloucester, that supplies electrified net fencing for any purpose such as protecting forestry, securing livestock, keeping cats or dogs in or out of gardens, and keeping foxes off bowling greens. The fencing is manufactured in various heights and the company (which is recommended by the Fox Project), will be happy to advise on the most appropriate kit of fencing, energiser and battery for use as a fox deterrent.

Foxes screaming

The Fox Project gets many complaints about the terrible noises made by foxes. They have an incredible range of calls, from the soft and gentle 'wo, wo, wo' to raucous screams which can chill the blood. Indeed many people are convinced that the screams are of cats being torn asunder by vicious foxes! In fact it is extremely rare, although not unknown, for any fox to get involved in a confrontation with a domestic cat. On the rare occasions there is such conflict it is normally either a dispute about territory and instigated by the cat, or a paranoid vixen defending its young cubs. After all, cats have been known to attack and kill very young fox cubs and adult foxes are devoted parents. However, with between 5,000 and 10,000 foxes living within the M25 motorway, if foxes regularly killed cats, London would soon be a cat-free zone! The common enemy of both the town cat and the town fox is the motor car. The difference is that foxes will happily scavenge squashed cats whereas cats would never stoop to eating foxes!

There is no way of stopping foxes screaming. In October when there is much competition between foxes for territory and in the mating period of January, many people will be awoken by bloodcurdling fox screams. Of course if you can deter them from your garden with Renardine or other repellents, then at least the noise may be more of a nuisance to your neighbours than to you. Personally, I love the sounds of foxes. It sends a pleasant sort of shiver down my spine, in the same way as the haunting howling of wolves. It's the call of the wild and you don't even have to get out of bed to hear it!

There are several ultrasound devices that are claimed to deter foxes and other animal nuisances. I have to say that I am not a great believer myself, but others report varying levels of success. The Fox Project reports success with a device called Animal Chaser made in Taiwan for Tensor Marketing Ltd of County Durham. Ultrasonic devices are supposed to work by introducing an annoying sound to the fox's environment, a sound that is above human hearing but which can be heard by animals. Apparently the ultrasound does not actually hurt the uninvited animal, but rather works like next door's music might affect us – 'it gets on your nerves'. I know of one ultrasonic 'scarer' set-up in a garden to repel foxes that was found the next morning to have been chewed into little pieces by the foxes! Whether this was because it was effective and they found it annoying, or whether it was ineffective and became an interesting 'squeaky' toy, we will never know! The manufacturers of some of these devices claim that they deter everything from ants to dogs. Some run off mains electricity and others are powered by batteries.

One device that I have found works brilliantly is a Canadian device called Scarecrow – imported and distributed by two or three UK companies. Until the year 2000 the device retailed at around £100 and was too expensive an option for many gardeners, but now at between £40 and £70 it is much more cost-effective. It connects to a garden hose and has a battery-powered infra-red detector which operates a valve so that any animal which comes within 35 feet receives a three-second burst of water from a sprinkler head. It can be moved around the lawn so that animals don't get used to its attack and I have found that it has deterred foxes that have defied all other repellents. Its disadvantages are that it can be triggered by shrubs moving in the wind, and that its effective range is too small for really large lawns. Obviously it cannot be used during frosty spells, but then foxes rarely cause damage during the hard part of winter.

Feeding foxes

If you like foxes and you want to attract them to your garden for the pure pleasure of seeing Britain's most beautiful mammal close-up, then by all means offer them a regular tit-bit or a mouthful of scraps or pet food. But it is unwise to be responsible for supplying the majority of your fox's dietary needs. Some people put out trays piled high with food and I have heard of one lady who gives 'her' fox a complete supermarket chicken every night. This is a mistake for several reasons. Firstly, if anything happens to you or you have to move away, your foxes will go hungry until they can learn to find other resources. But the second and less obvious reason for not being too generous to foxes is that the size of a fox's territory is largely dictated by the availability of food in that territory. If a fox obtains all it needs in your garden, why should it bother marking and defending a normal sized home range of 80 to 100 gardens. Other foxes will take over any undefended part of the territory, thereby increasing the population in the immediate area. This restricts your foxes to a territory of perhaps two or three gardens in which they and their offspring will have to spend their entire lives – sleeping, playing . . . and defecating.

I have been involved in several cases where disputes between neighbours have broken out because one person insists on putting out huge amounts of food for 'their' foxes, while all the fouling, digging and damage occurs in their immediate neighbours' gardens. A determined fox-lover might be prepared to put up with the resulting animosity, but unfortunately that animosity usually becomes directed at 'those bloody foxes'.

What we fox admirers want is for people to either share our affection for foxes or at least to be tolerant of them. The main reasons foxes have suffered so much cruelty and persecution over the centuries are ignorance and superstition. Now that scientists and television naturalists are effectively dispelling those negative factors, the last thing foxes need is to have people talking in bus queues, at check-outs, in workshops and in offices, about 'stinking foxes' wrecking their gardens. Such attitudes result in complaints to local authorities and 'pest' control companies being called in to trap and kill the 'pests' – all because a few unthinking enthusiasts insist on their right to lay out nightly banquets for 'their' foxes!

Squirrels

British population of breeding-age adults:
Grey squirrels 2.52 million
Red squirrels 160,000 mostly in Scotland.

Calendar (may vary)
January – Peak mating period.
February/March – Births of spring litters (average 3 per litter).
April – Young squirrels seen outside drey.
May – Young leave home and become independent.
July – Births of second litters while Spring young disperse.
September – Summer juveniles become independent.
October – Summer young disperse.
December – Females in oestrus at the end of the month.

You will be a very rare individual if a red squirrel causes you a problem. It is officially classified as one of Britain's rarest native mammals and fully protected by being listed in Schedule 5 of the Wildlife & Countryside Act 1981. For most of us the only squirrel we are likely to see in the lower two-thirds of Britain, and certainly the only one we will see in our suburban and urban gardens, is the grey – the American cousin of our native species.

Contrary to popular belief, grey squirrels do not kill reds and neither do they drive them out of the woods. Indeed greys and reds may not only share the same environment, but they have also been known to use the same dreys. It is also a fact that most of the remaining red squirrels in Britain are no more 'native' than the grey, as they are the descendants of red squirrels from Scandinavia and elsewhere, introduced following previous local extinctions of the true native reds.

Red squirrel populations have been declining for centuries for several reasons; firstly, climatic changes have resulted in the reds' true habitat, the great pine forests, retreating north and being replaced in southern Britain by broadleaf woodlands – the perfect habitat for greys. Secondly, millions of acres of woodlands have been destroyed over many centuries for agriculture, industry and housing; and thirdly, red squirrels have been ruthlessly persecuted by foresters and gamekeepers. In Scotland in the early 1900s clubs were set up to kill red squirrels;

one single club, the Highland Squirrel Club, killed 80,000 red squirrels in the first 30 years of its existence. In Hampshire's New Forest, red squirrels were still official- ly persecuted as 'pests' up until the late 1920s. On top of all that, 50 per cent of Britain's woodlands that survived the Second World War have been destroyed since. Living on the edge of its natural range, losing even its far-from-ideal habitat at a high rate, and being trapped and shot by humans, has subjected the red squirrel to so much stress that it has also become susceptible to out- breaks of disease – particularly parapoxvirus, which has symptoms similar to myxomatosis in rabbits. Some peo- ple have accused the grey squirrel of passing the disease on to reds, but the disease was killing red squirrels in areas before any grey squirrel had arrived. In 40 out of 44 districts where red squirrels were affected by the disease in the first 20 years of the twentieth century, no grey squirrel had ever set paw!

There is one way in which grey squirrels may have had a small adverse effect on the survival prospects of reds in some areas. One of the reasons reds managed to survive for so long in our broadleaf woodlands instead of their ideal pine forests, was because of the tradition of hazel coppicing. This managed method of timber production produced a hazel nut harvest which gave the red squirrels a food source on which to survive with little competition. However, in the late 1870s members of the aristocracy began to import and release grey squirrels from America. The most well-known introductions were at Woburn Park in 1889 and not only did the squirrels spread naturally from there, but they were also transported all over the country. The greys found plenty of food, including acorns upon which reds do not thrive, but also competed with the reds for hazel nuts. There was abundant food until the end of the Second World War, when the hazel coppicing industry virtually died out. Reds, therefore, found themselves in competition with greys for a diminishing food source and this may have accelerated the already inevitable demise of a viable population of red squirrels.

The damage inflicted on trees by grey squirrels, which is given as the excuse for their ruthless, pointless and ineffective persecution by man, is much exaggerated. True, grey squirrels strip bark during the mating period, but so do red squirrels. Such stripping rarely kills a tree and the only real economic damage is to beech and sycamore plantations grown to full maturity for the high quality timber trade. When a beech tree is cut down at 120 years old, aesthetically displeasing flaws may be found, which were caused by a squirrel having stripped off a piece of bark when the tree was only a couple of decades old.

There is no excuse for persecuting squirrels in amenity woodlands or in those grown for lower quality timber. Although squirrels occasionally steal bird eggs or even young chicks, there is no evidence to suggest that this predation has any impact on bird populations. Many grey squirrels live in towns and cities and, as with foxes, some people admire them and willingly encourage them to their gardens with food, while others curse them for digging in their plant tubs or stealing food from bird-tables. However, the only time squirrels can be an actual danger is when they gain access to our homes – usually lofts and roof spaces. I have seen electric cables completely stripped of insulation and of joists gnawed three-quarters through by squirrels that have set up home in a loft and built a cosy nest out of loft insulating material. There are also tales of squirrels drowning in water tanks – contaminating the water supply.

Fortunately, squirrels make so much noise thumping around in a loft that their occupation is rarely a secret. Driving them out is simple; one needs merely to climb into the loft during daylight hours, choosing a nice day if possible. The squirrels will probably be out foraging, but if you are nervous make plenty of noise as you climb in and you will find that the squirrels will have fled. Once inside, don't turn on any lights, and have a good look around. You may see a shaft of sunlight streaming in through the hole used for access by the squirrels.

The next step is to use a good torch to carefully check the entire loft space for any nests and whether such a nest contains baby squirrels – which could be present any time between February and August. If babies are present, merely disturb the nest a little and make it obvious that it has been visited. Leave something next to the nest that carries human odour or better still a towel which your cat or dog has slept on. With any luck the female squirrel will remove her babies one by one to another drey. They usually have two or three stand-by dreys to which they can move their family if they feel threatened.

If the squirrels refuse to leave or merely move their young to another part of your loft, it is best to wait until the youngsters are old enough to accompany their mother foraging outside. Get prepared with materials, be sure you know where the access hole is, and then watch for all the squirrels to go outside. If you leave it for a day or two while waiting for a local builder to carry out proper repairs, the squirrels will move back in. The best way of temporarily blocking out the squirrels is to fill the hole with expanding foam filler obtainable from any builders' merchants, or tightly wedge a piece of scrunched-up wire netting into the hole, and then staple more wire mesh over the area. But until you can have the area properly proofed you will need to check every day that the squirrels have not gnawed a new hole next to the blocked one.

Squirrels in the garden

As the famous television lager advertisement proves, squirrels are highly intelligent, very determined, and extremely athletic. If you wish to prevent squirrels stealing food you are putting out for birds, you will need to use plenty of imagination and ingenuity! (Personally, although I am no advocate of artificially feeding either wild birds or animals, I would get more pleasure from watching squirrels than blue tits.) If squirrels are climbing up the post of a bird table, you need to fit a metal or plastic skirt in the shape of a shallow cone around the post. Ideally it will need to be around one metre in diameter, but you may be able to adapt a plastic bowl. Squirrel-proof bird feeders are now available from garden centres, but they must be hung by strong metal wire as squirrels will gnaw through string or plastic and carry off the feeder to work on at their leisure!

Another method of preventing squirrels from eating food put out for birds is to mix capsicum pepper in with the food. It is claimed that this adds useful Vitamin A to the birds' diet, but is distasteful to squirrels and other mammals.

If you are siting a bird table or feeder then make sure that it is at least three metres from any tree branches or buildings from which squirrels can leap. If you have large trees near your house, it is also a good idea to keep branches at least three metres clear of the roof.

Squirrels will take strawberries, apples and plums and dig holes in the lawn to bury food. Conical plastic or metal skirts around trees may prevent the squirrels climbing, but ground fruit such as strawberries may have to be protected by a wire cage – which of course will also prevent birds from raiding the fruit. Plastic or string netting may keep off birds, but will not deter squirrels. Flapping strips of plastic tied to sticks may be enough to prevent serious damage from either birds or squirrels.

Squirrels often dig holes in plant tubs – either to bury food or to steal bulbs. Sprinkling Get Off My Garden crystals on the surface of the soil in the tub usually solves this problem. Holes in lawns should be filled in after dropping a few Get Off My Garden crystals into the hole and then spraying the lawn with Scoot or similar product usually puts an end to the problem.

If squirrels continue to cause you problems, try the Scarecrow device which detects intruders and squirts water at them or visit a good toy shop and invest in a powerful water-gun. These are highly effective weapons for ambushing any unwanted daylight visitor, wild or domestic, if you have the patience to sit and wait.

Moles

British population of breeding age adults – 31 million.

Breeding season – February to June (a month later in
    Scotland).

After 4-week gestation an average of four young born
    blind and naked.

June/July – young leave nest to explore tunnel system.
    At nine weeks old young emerge above ground and
    disperse.

Despite there being five times as many moles as rats,
most people have never seen a mole above ground and
know very little about this secretive subterranean creature. Consequently there is no Society for the Protection
of Moles, and the mole is the only British animal which

it is legal to kill with that most obscene of poisons – strychnine. This is a tragedy, not only for moles, but also for other wild animals and birds. I have heard it said that enough strychnine is sold every year to kill every British mole several times over, despite the fact that the poison can only be purchased by holders of a permit from one of three government agricultural departments. Moles are also preyed upon by owls, herons, buzzards, foxes, stoats and weasels, and many are killed, but not eaten, by domestic cats.

Most moles live in rural areas where some farmers ignore their activities while others regard even one molehill as a totally unacceptable invasion of their fields! Clearly a field covered in small heaps of soil, often containing small stones, can cause a lot of damage to mowing machinery, and silage made from grass contaminated with a lot of loose soil is unpalatable to livestock. Damage can also be caused to root crops and seedlings if moles disturb their roots while burrowing. On the other hand moles can be beneficial to farmers and gardeners because their tunnels aerate the soil and they prey on cockchafers and wireworms which damage crops.

As far as urban moles are concerned the main complaints arise when moles spoil grassy surfaces that we want flat and true, either for sporting activities such as golf, football, tennis or bowls, or for our garden lawns.

It is perfectly understandable that the owners or users of such grass get very angry when heaps of soil appear on the surface or the turf begins to sink and undulate due to tunnels just below the grass. However, considering that there is a breeding population of over 30 million moles in Britain, the damage they do is not nationally significant.

There are two types of tunnel. There are deep tunnels (up to 20 cm below the surface) and it is the soil from these that is pushed up to form the molehills. It is usually in these deep tunnels that the mole creates its nest for breeding or sleeping. There are also shallow tunnels just under the surface which create a ridge across the ground surface. The main function of a mole's burrow is to provide food. A mole needs to eat up to half its body weight every day and its tunnel system acts as a trap into which fall earthworms and insect larvae. As the mole patrols its tunnel its efficient senses of hearing and touch quickly detect such prey. Moles dig throughout the year, but once it has created a burrow extensive enough to provide it with sufficient food, it may stop digging and thus also stop creating molehills. Therefore if the main nuisance is the presence of molehills this may be solved, at least temporarily, by simply removing the heaps. However, during periods of cold weather moles have to extend their tunnels to find the dormant worms and insects, or dig deeper into the earth where the soil is warmer. This is why fresh molehills often appear in snow or frost. At the onset of the breeding season in late February male moles also significantly extend their tunnels.

One cannot estimate the size of a mole population by counting the molehills. There may only be a handful of molehills, but dozens of moles. On the other hand, depending on the weather, there may be dozens of molehills, but only a couple of moles under the surface. In November 1999, biologists at Imperial College, Silwood Park, Berkshire reported that two years of field tests had contradicted the theory that there are fewer molehills where earthworms are abundant. It had been believed that moles would dig less if their main food source was plentiful. In fact the research showed that where there are fewer earthworms there is less digging and thus fewer molehills.

Moles are largely solitary animals and, except for a brief period in the breeding season when males visit the territories of females, they will not tolerate another mole in their defended tunnel system. Tunnel systems do overlap, but the residents try to avoid conflict by trying not to be in the same place at the same time. However it is known that there are what seem to be 'communal' tunnels which several moles will use, often to reach water, particularly in periods of drought.

The size of individual territories depends on the type of habitat, the season and the sex of the mole. Males have territories ranging from 3,000 square metres (summer) to 7,000 square metres during the breeding season. Females' territories are around 2,000 square metres at all times of the year.

If a mole is killed or otherwise removed from its territory, another mole will take over the vacant territory within hours.

So what should one do if one has moles spoiling one's lawn? Golf clubs and bowling greens minimise mole damage by treating the land with worm killers (lumbricides). This treatment not only results in a habitat not capable of supporting moles, but also creates a surface unspoilt by worm casts. This somewhat drastic and ethically dubious treatment can also be applied to lawns to deter occupation by moles, but if a lawn is bereft of earthworms it will need more maintenance such as spiking to replace the beneficial aeration normally provided by the worms. Only products specifically approved by the Department for the Environment, Food and Rural Affairs (DEFRA) as lumbricides can be used. The research at Imperial College in Berkshire mentioned above suggests that lowering the soil's pH by not applying lime treatments will decrease earthworm abundance and therefore decrease mole activity.

Some garden centres sell a product called Mole Away, manufactured from inert castor oil which, it is claimed, will keep moles away from a lawn for periods up to ten weeks per sprayed application. Renardine is also an approved repellent for moles. The liquid is soaked into small pieces of rag that are then poked down into the moles tunnels – the idea being that the strong smell drives the mole away.

As well as mole traps which kill the animal, there are others which can be placed in a mole's tunnel and capture it unharmed. These traps must be checked frequently as moles cannot survive long without food; I would recommend checking at least four times a day and if possible once or twice at night by torch light. Captured moles can be released in deciduous woodland or on permanent pasture if the owners don't mind. However, moles are notoriously shy of traps and may merely dig a tunnel around any strange object that appears in the tunnel.

In my view the most logical approach to persuading a troublesome mole to leave a lawn is to treat its tunnel with some pungent smell that the animal finds unpleasant and that may interfere with its detection of its prey. However, such a tactic may have the very opposite effect. All animals are individuals, and individuals react differently when confronted with the same circumstances. Finding its tunnel system inhospitable may cause a mole to leave and possibly travel far enough to resolve the problem. On the other hand the mole may merely dig a new tunnel system, thus doubling the number of unsightly molehills!

I was recently contacted by a gardener in France whose large lawns were being badly disfigured by moles. He tried every repellent he could find – without success. He even resorted to inserting poisons into the tunnels; still no success. I advised him that by continually fouling the moles' tunnels, he could well have been exacerbating the problem by provoking them into digging more 'clean' tunnels. I suggested he should first try removing all the mole heaps to establish whether the moles were still digging or whether they had created a big enough tunnel system to meet their needs.

When trying to repel moles from a lawn, the first consideration is whether there is adjacent habitat such as pasture or woodland to which the mole can move. If so, then fouling the tunnels may solve your problem. There are dozens of ways of fouling mole tunnels . . . and not just with smells. Some gardeners swear that pushing the stick of a child's windmill down into the tunnel causes moles to leave. There was once such a device called Dynamole that transferred the resonance from the rotating mill down through an amplifying tube into the subsoil. By using several such Dynamoles in a sweeping pattern, the idea was to persuade the moles to leave the area. I don't know how successful the Dynamole was, but perhaps a clue is that it is no longer produced. A similar device is the Sonic Mole Chaser, produced by the Pestcontro company, who claim that ten of the 'chasers' solved a mole infestation at the Royal Stables of the United Arab Emirates. The company also claims that the vibration produced by the device is equally effective against shrews, voles, ground squirrels, pocket mice and gophers – not that there are many of the last three species in the UK!

Some people claim that sinking bottles into the lawn so that the wind blows across the top of the bottle causing a vibration is effective. Garden centres sell devices that are supposed to interfere with the earth's magnetic field and thus repel moles, and some people claim that ultra-sound devices work. One traditional method of repelling moles is laying prickly vegetation such as holly leaves in the moles' tunnels. The pest control manual of ADAS (Agriculture Development and Advisory Service) mentions the above repellent devices and traditional methods, but dismisses them as being of '*equally doubtful effectiveness*'.

If it is decided to use chemicals to repel moles, remember that it is an offence to use any chemical for any purpose other than that for which it has been approved.

If it does not make it clear on the can or bottle that it can be used as a repellent for moles, *then don't use it*. Some people insert mothballs into mole tunnels, not realising that it is a criminal offence to use mothballs for this purpose. Mothballs are for dealing with moths – nothing else. They contain naphthalene, which if ingested by dogs can cause anaemia and if swallowed by children can turn their urine red! Even minute amounts of naphthalene can cause Vitamin A deficiency in cattle – leading to thickening of the skin, eye discharges, frothing of the mouth, and emaciation.

When I was living in Somerset in the late 1960s, I awoke one morning to find my small front lawn covered in molehills. After removing the heaps of soil, I collected up the contents of a couple of ashtrays and poked the smelly dog-ends down into the tunnels – cork tip and all. I even blew cigarette smoke down the tunnels, working on the principle that only human beings are silly enough to enjoy tobacco smoke and that even smokers (I no longer am) find the smell of ashtrays and stubbed-out cigarettes unpleasant. It may be coincidence, but the mole left without creating any more hills. Another possible solution was once recommended by Nigel Colborn, a regular panellist on BBC Radio 4's Gardener's Question Time. He suggested placing a 'singing birthday card' down a mole tunnel as an effective deterrent, explaining that it plays a tune for weeks and the mole can't stand the noise!

Rabbits

British adult population: 37 million.

Main breeding season: January–July.

Females can breed at 4–5 months old.

Gestation period: 28–30 days.

Average 5 young per litter. 4–5 litters per year.

Introduced into Britain in the twelfth century, rabbits were kept in huge warrens to provide human food. The inevitable escapes led eventually to rabbits becoming the countryside's most common mammal; by the 1950s there were at least 60 million of the animals causing agricultural damage estimated at £120 million annually. In 1953 the horrendous disease myxomatosis was deliberately introduced into Britain and with the virus rapidly being spread by the rabbit flea, within a few years 99.99 per cent of rabbits had died. However, the 0.01 per cent that survived the disease thereafter were immune and by the 1960s between 5 per cent and 30 per cent were surviving new outbreaks.

By the mid-1970s scientists discovered that genetic resistance (as opposed to immunity) was occurring in baby rabbits and now, at 37 million and rising, rabbits are rapidly on their way back to the pre-myxomatosis population levels. Had it not been for the continuing persecution of predators such as foxes, stoats and weasels by farmers and gamekeepers, the rabbit population once decimated by disease may have been kept low by natural predators. Scientific research conducted by the Ministry of Agriculture, Fisheries and Food (as it then was) in the 1980s suggests that when rabbit numbers are low, natural predators can help prevent rapid expansion of the rabbit population, but where predators are persecuted by man rabbits are significantly more widespread and abundant.

The disease was perhaps a turning point in rural history as up until then rabbit was the only affordable meat for thousands of farmers and rural folk. The deliberate introduction of the horrific disease and the rapid demise of rabbits not only deprived many humans of meat, but also impacted on many predators such as buzzards, stoats and weasels. Foxes too had to switch to field voles for their staple diet. Another effect of the loss of rabbits was that areas of downland where grazing by large populations of rabbits had kept grass short and allowed orchids and many other plants to grow, became overgrown with long grass and scrub. I remember well as a boy that Ham Hill, a local beauty spot near my home town of Yeovil, lost its popularity with families as a place to visit on Sundays, because without rabbits the previously shorn carpet of grass became long and rank and overgrown with brambles.

It is, of course, true that rabbits can cause economic losses to farming through eating crops and competing with livestock for grass, but myxomatosis was such a horrible disease that any satisfaction felt by farmers was soon reversed by the widespread and horrific sight of rabbits blindly stumbling about in country lanes, their heads swollen and leaking pus. The outcry in the country as a whole was so great that Winston Churchill's government insisted on adding a clause to the Pests Act 1954 making it a criminal offence to use infected rabbits to spread myxomatosis.

Rabbits are largely confined to the countryside, but can invade gardens of houses on the edge of the town. They may also cause problems on golf courses, bowling greens and sports fields. The most efficient way to keep rabbits out of one's garden or perhaps part of it, is the erection of permanent fencing. It should have a mesh size of not more than 31mm and consist of at least 19 gauge wire. The fence should be not less than 100 cms high

and there needs to be at least 15 cms of the mesh turned out at right angles at the bottom and pegged to the ground to prevent the rabbits digging under the fence. This apron can either be covered with soil, or grass could be allowed to grow through it. It is important that the fence has enough posts to keep the wire tight and prevent sagging.

Tinsley Wire Products, based in Sheffield, manufacture Sentinel Green Rabbit Proof Netting and produce a helpful booklet entitled *Fencing to prevent damage to crops and trees by rabbits*. Fencing may seem expensive, but it should last about 10 years if properly erected.

Renardine liquid repellent is also an approved rabbit repellent and can either be mixed with sand and spread around the area to be protected, or bundles of sticks or rags can be soaked in the liquid and used as a barrier. The disadvantages of Renardine are that it has a very strong creosote-type smell, will require regular renewal, will 'burn' or discolour grass, and must not be allowed to get into ponds as it harms fish and amphibians.

A 'greener' way of protecting a small vegetable bed is to surround it with dried gorse or holly leaves, sprinkled liberally in a 50 cms wide band around the area to be protected. The idea is that the rabbits will find the prickles too sharp for their feet. Some people claim that a border of rue (*Ruta graveolens*) acts as a deterrent, while others swear that human urine will keep rabbits off. There are many attractive garden flowers which rabbits avoid, including yellow flag, cyclamen foxglove, snow-drops, daffodils and scarlet pimpernel. If you are planning a hedge, you may find it useful to know that box, rhododendron and laurel and clematis are all avoided by rabbits.

Rats and Mice

Breeding age population: Rats 6.8 million; House Mice 5.2 million.

Sexually mature at 3 months.

Gestation period: Rat 21–24 days; House Mouse 17–20 days.

Litter size   Rat 6–11; House Mouse 5–6.

To all intents and purposes there is now only one rat in Britain – the Common rat, sometimes called the Norway, Sewer or Brown rat. The estimated population of adult breeding Common rats is less than seven million. Claims in tabloid newspapers that there as many rats as humans and that each British citizen is never more than a few yards away from a rat, are nonsense, as are many myths perpetuated about rats; for instance that when cornered they go for your throat! In November 2000 a national newspaper accepted and published without question the claim that during the summer there had been a 31 per cent rise in the number of rats to at least 58 million. The newspaper warned that in major cities you are never more than 20 metres from a rat.

Yet, five years previously in June 1995, another newspaper had claimed that there were already 60 million rats in Britain having increased by 39 per cent in 14 years!

A year earlier, in September 1994, yet another newspaper claimed that the British rat population had reached 56 million, having increased by 39 per cent in the previous year alone! Clearly, it is not possible for all the above 'facts' to be true.

The language used by the media commonly denigrates rats as filthy, prolific, ravenous, dangerous and vicious. One newspaper reported a tale from China where it was claimed that thousands of rats had committed suicide by diving into a lake because there wasn't enough food to feed them all, another claimed that rats in Iran had eaten a five month old baby and that in the Middle Ages rats' fleas spread the Black Death that killed up to half of Europe's population. What the paper did not mention that the rats which were responsible for the plague were Black rats, now rare in Britain, and that unlike the Common brown rat, the Black or Ship rat commonly lived in roofs and rooms of human dwellings rather than the sewers, drains and ditches more normally inhabited by the Common brown species. Pest controllers who rely for their business on the perpetration of such scare stories must have been rubbing their hands with glee. In fact there are seven species of British mammals more numerous than rats; the Pygmy shrew, 8.6 million; Bank vole, 23 million; mole, 31 million; rabbit, 37 million; Wood mouse, 38 million; Common shrew, 41.7 million and Field vole, 75 million.

The Black rats' population is down as low as 1,300 adults which, in terms of a rodent that has lived in Britain since the third century AD and was once the dominant rat species, is virtual extinction. It says a lot about our historical experience of the Black rat and its role in the plague, that conservationists have not raised as much as a whisper about the fact that such a formerly prolific mammal is facing extinction.

There are still thought to be a handful of Black rats living in port buildings at Tilbury, Liverpool and Avonmouth, whereas the Common or Brown rat thrives in both rural and urban areas and is often associated with sewers where it feeds on our waste. I once read that without rats poking about for food and breaking up the jams of sewage that clog up at pipe junctions, the sewers would soon overflow into the streets of our major towns and cities – or maybe that is just another myth about rats. There are many. For instance, one well-worn fable is that two rats will work together to steal a chicken's egg. One rat is reputed to grasp the egg between all four legs and then roll onto its back. Then the second rat grips its partner's tail in its mouth and uses its colleague as a sledge to drag the egg safely out of the hen-house and under the wire.

Another common country story is that the storyteller was pedalling his bike home in the dark after closing time, when he was confronted with the sight and sound of hordes of squeaking rats blanketing the road as they marched to a new farm having laid bare their home farm's food supplies. Invariably the story-teller had to drop his bike and hastily clamber up a tree rather than risk being overwhelmed and left behind as a skeleton by the hungry rats. A great tale, and of course impossible to disprove!

In urban areas the main concerns associated with rats and mice, are damage to sewers from burrowing, to electricity cables and lead pipes caused by gnawing, contamination of stored food and the risk of disease. The most talked-about disease associated with rats is Weil's Disease, a type of leptospirosis. In the UK the bacterium has been found in the kidneys of more than a third of the rats in sampled rat populations. Infected rats shed the bacterium in their urine, but do not appear to suffer harm themselves. The bacterium can only survive outside the

rat's body in wet environments and therefore is usually transmitted to humans by contact with contaminated water or moist soil – the organism entering the human body through cuts or abrasions or the mucous membranes of the nose and mouth. It used to be only workers in agriculture, sewers and abattoirs that were affected, but with the increase in water sports, there has been a rise in the number of cases amongst swimmers, water skiers and canoeists.

Weil's Disease is a notifiable disease and in humans can range in severity from flu-like symptoms to jaundice, renal failure and even death. However, the numbers of people who suffer from the disease is relatively small. It should also be borne in mind that in some areas it has been found that 40 per cent of domestic dogs have at some time been infected and it is known that dogs which recover from a bout of leptospirosis may excrete the organism for up to a further 18 months! For obvious reasons leptospirosis used to be commonly referred to as 'the lamp-post disease'.

The other main disease of practical significance to humans in the UK is salmonellosis, a type of food poisoning sometimes resulting from the contamination of food and drink with rodent excreta. In humans the symptoms include gastroenteritis accompanied by headache, fever and vomiting.

To avoid sharing our homes and workplaces with

rodents we need to ensure that there is never any food available to attract their attention, and that as far as possible we deny access to any rodents looking for a safe refuge in which to live and rear their young. Once they do gain entry, getting them out again can be extremely difficult. The first step is to discover where the animals have gained entry and to plan ahead on sealing off such access once you have evicted your unwelcome visitors. Mice can squeeze through a gap less than 10 mm wide and are excellent climbers. Rats may gain access to a building through drains and set up home within a hollow wall. Check for broken air vents and for gaps around pipes that go through walls.

Rodents can be prevented using tree branches as a route to roofs and walls by keeping such branches cut back. Similarly a large metal disc fitted as a barrier will prevent most rats (and squirrels) using cables as a 'high-wire' to human habitation. Fitting metal cone guards around drainpipes, (wide end of the cone facing downwards and a perimeter of at least 250 mm out from the pipe) will prevent rodents climbing up between the pipe and the wall. However, remember that rats can sometimes climb up the inside of drainpipes and therefore it would also be wise to fit a metal mesh balloon guard at the top of the pipe. This will allow rainwater to run into the pipe from the guttering but will prevent rodents climbing up and out of the pipe.

Where rats or mice come and go regularly you may see dark smears caused by the natural grease and dirt rubbing off the animals' fur. You may find food, packaging or cables gnawed by the rodents. If the parallel grooves caused by the incisor teeth are about 3 mm wide, then you have rats, and if only 1 mm then you are host to House mice. Rat droppings are on average 12 mm long and tapering to a point at one or both ends, whereas House mouse droppings are 3–7 mm long.

Rats and mice tend to use regular routes and will leave recognisable trails. Rat runs outside will appear as narrow, well-worn, bare earth paths, and inside the trails can often be seen as clear bands through dust.

Mice are comparatively easy to capture in humane 'trip traps' of which there are many examples available in hardware stores and garden centres. Larger cage traps are also available for capturing rats, but they are notoriously trap shy and you may need to bait the trap for many days or even weeks before the rats brave the 'new' object in their territory.

There are two problems with live trapping. Firstly, what if the rodents have a nest full of young that will starve to death if you remove their mother? Secondly, what do you do with the trapped animals?

If you know where the rats or mice are located you could try to expose the place to see if there is a nest with young. The exposure may well persuade the mother to move her young although of course she may move them to another inaccessible place. Or you could try to remove the entire nest with its young intact and place it outside near the adults' entry point, in the hope that the mother will relocate her family elsewhere. However, the parents may well abandon the nest and their young. All animals are individuals and one can never be exactly sure how they will react. There are no simple fail-safe solutions in such circumstances – one can only do one's best.

If you feel that you have to take some action and as a result find yourself left with a nest full of baby rodents on your hands, you could try to find a local wildlife rescue centre that will agree to take them in and hand-rear them (yes, some will help rats and mice as well as the more 'acceptable' wildlife), or you could take them along to a veterinary surgery, RSPCA or PDSA clinic (none of whom would agree to rear rats or mice) and ask them to humanely destroy the animals.

Once you have captured your rats or mice, the problem arises as to where best to release them. With mice, if you have or know of an old shed at the bottom of the garden, you could drop them off there – ideally with some corn or other food to give them a start in their new home. With captured rats, I recommend that they be dropped off in dense woodland. Realistically, they will probably soon fall prey to foxes or owls, but rats have so many enemies and predators that it is rare for them to survive more than eight months – no matter where they live.

You may find that you have rats living in your garden. Again some detective work needs to be carried out to discover why they have chosen the location. Very often the attraction will be a nearby bird table or feeders; or someone may be throwing out bread for pigeons; or perhaps the compost heap is the attraction. The rats' burrows may be in sloping ground or in ditches, or under logs, paving stones or tree roots. The holes are 70 to 120 mm in diameter and the burrows may well link up with a drain or sewer.

Once you have dealt with the food source, the rats will probably move off to find another fast food outlet. But to help persuade them to move on, ensure as few hiding places as possible, keep vegetation cut right down and crop grass short as rats don't like to cross open ground. Wherever you see a rat run, place an object on it. It could be just a stone or a lump of wood. Next day move the objects somewhere else on the run, or dig up a part of the trail. Rats are very sensitive to changes in their environment. Disturbance and new objects could spell danger! Raising their anxiety level may well be enough to persuade them to vacate the area.

It should be remembered that rodent colonies defend their territories against intrusion by other members of the same species. As the population increases in the territory high-ranking individuals suppress the feeding and breeding opportunities of lower-ranking animals. This has the effect of limiting population numbers in an area. In House mice, when the population reaches a certain level, aggressive behaviour increases and low-ranking mice are unable to hold territory and therefore will not breed.

It is clear therefore that the most important precaution we can take is to be meticulous about food wastage. Make sure all waste bins have their lids firmly in place. Never leave food out in plastic bags. Remember that if you put out food to encourage wildlife, you will also attract scavengers and the predators of the wildlife you are seeking to encourage!

Badgers

British population of breeding age adults: 250,000.

Calendar

Mating – Normally July, but can be any time between
February and October.

January–March – Cubs (1–5) born 7 to 8 weeks after de-
layed implantation of the embryo.

March–May – Cubs appear above ground.

Winter – Badgers spend most of their time in their under-
ground setts.

Badgers are not generally considered to be urban dwellers, but where town meets country, particularly where
there is woodland and pasture, badgers may occasionally
cause problems if they dig their setts beneath roads,

buildings or gardens. Their nocturnal foraging for earthworms and insect larvae can also severely damage lawns, crops, and amenities such as golf courses. Badgers may also be attracted by food scraps put out for birds, are adept at removing lids from dustbins and will sometimes raid strawberry crops and dig out carrots and other root vegetables.

Such damage can occasionally be confused with that inflicted by foxes, and even deer. It is important therefore to establish either by observation or detective work, exactly which species is the culprit. Badgers pushing under fences, particularly barbed wire, leave hairs that are quite distinctive, with a black middle section and light tip. The hairs are coarse and do not roll easily between one's finger and thumb. Other badger signs are their loose droppings deposited in small holes or 'dung-pits'. The pits are often used as territory markers to indicate the group's boundary and the droppings are loose and messy due to the soil in the badgers' favourite diet of earthworms, but in the autumn fruit stones and cereals may also be evident.

Badger setts may consist of a single hole or an extensive labyrinth of tunnels with many exits. Unlike foxes, badgers collect ferns, straw, hay and leaves for bedding and regularly change it, leaving the discarded bedding outside the main entrance to the sett in amongst soil regularly scraped out to keep the tunnels clear. This spoil heap is a sure sign that the hole is or has been used by badgers and it is important to remember that badger setts in current use, as well as the badgers themselves, are protected by the law. It is an offence to interfere with a badger sett – 'interference' being defined as damage, destruction, obstructing access to entrances, causing dogs to enter, or disturbance of a badger when it is in occupation.

Under the Protection of Badgers Act 1992 it is an offence to wilfully kill, injure or take a badger or attempt to do so; importantly, it is also an offence to cruelly ill-treat any badger, and therefore anyone experiencing problems with badgers would be well advised to seek expert advice before taking any action. Such advice can be obtained from local badger protection groups, ADAS wildlife consultants, the Department of the Environment, Food and Rural Affairs (DEFRA), English Nature, Countryside Council for Wales, Scottish Natural Heritage, the Scottish Office, Agriculture and Fisheries Department and Welsh Office Agriculture Department

Where necessary, licences for interference with setts and badgers can be issued by government agriculture or conservation departments, but such licences are only granted in serious cases and almost certainly never during the period from 1 December to 30 June, the badgers' main breeding season. However there are harmless actions that can be taken in an attempt to prevent badgers from damaging gardens or deter them from places where they are unwanted. Electric fencing (not netting, in which badgers could become entangled) is an effective barrier. Approved chemical repellents such as Renardine can be soaked into sand that can be spread on the badger's preferred paths, in the hope that they will divert their nightly patrols, and repellents such as Scoot or Get Off My Garden can be used on lawns and flower beds to mask the scent of earthworms and insect larvae in the soil.

However, with badgers being so highly protected, I recommend seeking expert advice before taking *any action at all*. The penalties for illegal ill-treatment of badgers are severe and can include both heavy fines and custodial sentences. Don't be misled by the fact that foxhunters have an exemption in the law which allows them to be the only people allowed to interfere with a badger sett by blocking it up on hunt days to prevent foxes using the holes to escape from the hounds. The Protection of Badgers Act 1992 began life as a Private Member's Bill presented by Welsh Labour Member of Parliament Roy Hughes in an effort to keep hunters with terriers away from badger setts. The Bill was presented in 1990/91 during the term of the Conservative Government and the parliamentary fox hunting lobby threatened to halt the bill's progress unless fox hunts were granted an exemption from prosecution for blocking setts. And do not be misled also by the fact that the Labour Government is presently (2002) engaged on the slaughter of up

20,000 badgers in the West Country to placate farmers who mistakenly believe that badgers are responsible for transmitting Bovine Tuberculosis to cattle. Of course when the slaughter was being carried out under a Conservative Government, Labour MPs vowed to 'save the badger' from such persecution. When those Labour MPs became the Government, their attitude changed and far from being stopped, the slaughter has dramatically increased as part of an appallingly unscientific experiment to finally discover whether badgers are implicated in the continuing and persistent presence of TB in cattle.

The MAFF (now DEFRA) badger culling programme has been in effect for more than a quarter of a century and yet it has failed to eliminate the disease in cattle. Officials admit that after all those years in which some disgustingly cruel experiments have been conducted, there is still only 'circumstantial evidence' that badgers transmit TB to cows. Eighty per cent of the badgers killed have been found not be infected with TB at all, and the disease has increased in cattle in areas where there is no TB in local badger populations. The theory is that the cattle ingest TB baccilli while grazing pasture contaminated by badger urine or excreta, but it is extremely rare for badgers to be so grossly infected with TB that they excrete infectious material. It is known that transmission of TB is normally through the respiratory system and rarely through the digestion system. Cows are

unlikely to eat grass so contaminated with infectious urine or faeces that it poses a disease threat.

The easiest transmission route for TB is through inhalation and there are not many people who claim to have seen sick badgers wandering round fields blowing up cows' noses! However, anyone who knows anything about cows knows that cows do blow up each other's noses as a vital component of social communication. It seems obvious to me that many cows are kept in high stocking densities and live highly stressful lives being continually robbed of their new-born calves so that we humans can take their milk. It is small wonder they are vulnerable to a disease like tuberculosis. One day, I am sure, it will be proved that badgers first contracted TB from the contaminated slurry and cow pats spread all over the pastures in the comparatively warm and damp South West of England and on which badgers forage (and breathe) for hours at a time. I am confident that it will also be proved that badgers have never had anything to do with transmitting the disease back to cattle, and that countless thousands of these inoffensive wild animals will have died for nothing.

The fact that the Badger Protection Act is, in practice, of so little protection to badgers provides even more reason why the rest of us should be as tolerant as possible and obey both the spirit and letter of badger protection legislation.

Deer

Deer are rarely a problem in urban areas but, like badgers, they can visit gardens on the edge of town. Only two species are worth mentioning in this context, the native Roe and the introduced Muntjac (or Barking) deer. The Roe deer is around 76 cms at the shoulder and the Muntjac is around 40 cms. Both are small enough to remain hidden in suburban gardens and the first sign of their presence may be destroyed roses – apparently much loved by all species of deer. Roe deer browse predominantly on leaves, but also eat grass, fungi, berries, acorns and beechmast in winter. They also bite off the tips of tree shoots and fray bark with their antlers. Muntjac too eat fruit and indulge in bark stripping.

The best defence against deer is permanent fencing which for Roe and Muntjac needs to be 1.5 m high with no gaps underneath, as deer will attempt to push under fences if they are too high to jump. Electric wire fencing is an alternative, but sheep netting should *not* be used as deer can become entangled in it and be tortured to death by the electric pulse. ADAS advises that electric fencing should only be seen as a short-term solution as Roe deer in particular are not easily deterred.

Plastic netting and metal guards can be used to protect small trees, but need to be 1.2 m high to prevent browsing. Chemical repellents such as Renardine are also approved for the deterrence of deer, but may be less effective than scarers such as flapping plastic ribbons and the Scarecrow water squirting device designed to repel a variety of mammals and birds. However, wild animals and birds cannot survive without using all their physical attributes and intelligence. Strange smells, noises and sights can cause them to avoid such worrying phenomena, but if the danger stands between them and a desirable food source or some other benefit, they will eventually test it. A piece of flapping plastic ribbon may deter a deer from raiding rose bushes for a night or two, but the deterrent effect will soon fade. Thus, if it is not possible to physically fence out the unwanted wildlife, considerable human ingenuity will be required to repeatedly change the nature of repellents to keep the intruders away.

Bats

All species of bats and their roosts are strictly protected by law and may only be disturbed or handled by licensed experts. Fortunately bats are harmless and anyone who finds that these vulnerable creatures have inhabited their roof space or loft, can rest assured that the bats will cause no damage to cables or roof timbers, and represent no risk to human health. According to ADAS the only slight problem that can be caused by bats in a loft is if, due to dampness, mould forms on their normally dry powdery droppings. This can lead to staining of ceilings, but clearly the problem is the dampness, not the bats.

Anyone who is concerned about bats in their property, or is contemplating any procedure such as woodworm treatment or installing a loft conversion where bats are present, must seek advice from a statutory conservation

B.SMALL

71

body, the Bat Conservation Trust, or wildlife consultant before taking action. Under the Wildlife & Countryside Act 1981, penalties for unlicensed disturbance or for causing harm to bats are severe.

Birds

Birds: A General Note

The British have a very strange attitude to birds. The result is that we have legislation that in theory protects all birds, but which permits:

- the breeding and release into the countryside of up to 40 million foreign birds (pheasants) every year to be shot for 'sport';
- the unmonitored killing of British native birds that shooters consider to be predators of their game birds;
- falconers to ignore European laws that prohibit the keeping of wild birds of prey in captivity for falconry;
- keeping captured wild birds in cages to act as decoys to attract other wild birds into traps – a criminal offence if it was done to attract mammals!

- poisoning countless thousands of feral pigeons that are direct descendants of the Rock dove (a protected species) and yet permitting people to feed feral pigeons in city centres!

Everybody loves songbirds and yet some gardeners still spread poisons around their gardens, particularly slug pellets, despite the clear evidence that such poisons have been implicated in the catastrophic decline of birds such as song thrushes. We allow the unrestricted ownership and breeding of cats that probably kill at least 100 million birds annually, while many people prefer to blame magpies for the decline of songbirds despite the fact that scientific research has vindicated the species.

In the Canadian state of Alberta, bylaws not only prohibit the keeping of more than two cats per household, but also insist that cats are not allowed out of their owner's garden unless on a lead. When I visited Calgary in September of 2000, I discovered that the bylaws were so very well respected that there had been a noticeable increase in garden songbirds. There are 85,000 cats in the city and yet on my 16-day visit to the city, I saw only two cats in the open air.

I doubt whether any politician, national or local, would dare suggest the adoption of such bylaws for Great Britain, but the protection of wildlife is of paramount importance to most Canadians. Here, conservationists continue to obstruct any proposal to build houses on the designated 'green belt', despite the fact that most of this 'belt' is in most cases virtually useless as wildlife habitat, and certainly much less useful than mature suburban gardens. Much green belt consists of huge fields of sterile grass grown to feed livestock and is devoid of the wild flowers and herbage needed to sustain bird life. The creation of villages and hamlets in these green belts, and restrictions on the more dangerous garden pesticides, would soon bring new colour and variation of flora to thousands of square kilometres of soulless land – as well as providing desperately needed human housing.

That all said, it is a fact that as with wild mammals, wild and feral birds can cause problems to us humans – even if in most cases it is human behaviour that can be found at the root of the problem; for instance with pigeons.

Pigeons

The large populations of feral pigeons in our towns and cities are sustained almost entirely by food discarded either carelessly or deliberately by human beings. The feral pigeon is a descendent of the rock dove – a protected species adapted for life on the inaccessible ledges of cliff faces – hence the pigeons' obvious comfort on the ledges of city office blocks. New blood is added to the flocks from the ranks of the large racing pigeon population – some of which opt for freedom or merely go astray.

Competition for food and nesting sites is intense – the size of the flocks being proportional to the amount of available food, although only a third of the population breeds. More than 40 per cent of the fledged young die each year, but this huge mortality is balanced by the fact that young pigeons are capable of breeding at only 5 months old.

Every summer in the media silly season a tabloid newspaper can be relied upon to dedicate a page or two to the latest pigeon controversy. The term 'flying rats' will be used, together with a list of terrible diseases with which pigeons threaten us poor humans, or how the great buildings of London will soon be reduced to rubble by the corrosive action of tons of pigeon droppings, or how pensioners with broken hips are cluttering up NHS hospitals after slipping and sliding on pavements swimming in pigeon droppings.

There is, of course, a smattering of unspectacular truth behind such tales, but compared with the diseases, filth and vandalism inflicted upon us by members of our own species, pigeons hardly rate a mention. True, pigeon droppings erode masonry, but so do exhaust fumes and acid rain. The cost of cleaning Nelson's Column every other year, the daily washing of Trafalgar Square and changing the water in the fountains every 3 weeks, amounts to hundreds of thousands of pounds annually. Yet despite such costs and the fact that in theory pigeons are capable of transmitting 30 diseases to man, the feeding of corn to the famous pigeons has long been officially encouraged. The fact is the pigeons have always been recognised as a major tourist attraction. And tourists represent a huge economic benefit to London and the nation – dwarfing the costs of pigeon damage. After all, if pigeons really constituted the risk to human health that the tabloids claim in their annual scare stories, London hospitals would be full every summer with Japanese tourists struck down with avian diseases.

In September 2000, the newly elected Mayor of London, Ken Livingstone, declared that the licensed sale of pigeon food in Trafalgar Square was to end, in an effort to rid the Square of the pigeons. His announcement resulted in protests from animal rights groups, but Mr Livingstone went on to declare publicly that pigeons were just 'rats with wings' – a comment which did little to quell the protests. As I write, the licensed sale of corn in the Square has ended and activists are providing alternative food supplies for the birds. Whatever the outcome of the controversy, pigeons will no doubt continue to be a popular feature of Trafalgar Square.

There have been many such local newsworthy battles and rows over pigeons. A few people who have created a public nuisance by insisting on feeding copious amounts of bread to the birds, despite protests from neighbours and appeals by local Council officials, have found themselves in court and even in gaol for insisting that they have the right to feed the birds whenever and wherever they wish. On the other hand blinkered Council environmental health officers have provoked numerous animal rights demonstrations following Council attempts to rid an area of pigeons by use of lethal weapons such as air rifles and poisons.

The simple fact is that methods of pigeon control have been largely unsuccessful due to a lack of understanding of the species. Towns and cities the world over have tried to control numbers of pigeons using a wide variety of methods including lethal control, trapping and deterrents. All these methods have not only failed to reduce the numbers of birds in the long term, but have also involved a considerable waste of financial resources – to say nothing of the infliction of varying degrees of unnecessary suffering to the birds and the genuine distress of many bird lovers.

In areas where lethal control has been tried, it has been found that within weeks, pigeon numbers have been fully restored to the pre-cull figure and possibly exceeded it. This is because killing adult birds leads to less competition in a feeding flock – thus favouring the survival of the younger, healthy birds which then become the new breeding stock.

Pigeons control their own populations very effectively according to the food source available to them. If conditions allow, a pair of pigeons can breed up to six times a year, producing two young each time. However, if the food supply is dramatically reduced the birds may not breed at all. Thus, problems with overpopulation of pigeons in towns and cities are caused by people providing too much food. If the public could be educated to phase out or reduce their pigeon feeding habits, there would be a huge decrease in pigeon numbers.

The solution to such pigeon problems has been effectively demonstrated in Switzerland. In 1988 and 1990 the city of Basel introduced a massive public information campaign to educate the public about pigeons and the relationship between feeding and overpopulation. At the time the city had a population of around 20,000 pigeons which had remained at that level despite the slaughter of 100,000 birds over the preceding 24 years. Alongside the education campaign the University of Basel was asked to conduct a scientific study to find a solution to the problem of overpopulation of pigeons in the city.

The end result was that the city authority, while upholding bylaws designed to discourage the feeding of pigeons, provided nine special designated feeding areas where members of the public could legitimately feed the pigeons. Adjacent to these areas they built well-kept and controlled pigeon lofts where the pigeons could nest and roost. These lofts were visited every day and any eggs removed during the four-year research period. The result was not only that the city's pigeon population was halved, but large quantities of pigeon droppings were deposited in the lofts that would otherwise have been spread around the city. The droppings could then be safely removed without inconvenience.

This simple and highly effective method of pigeon control has now been tried by a handful of British local authorities at the prompting of Guy Merchant who from his role as Project Manager of CARES Wildlife Hospital in Cambridgeshire, founded PICAS (Pigeon Control Advisory Service). PICAS persuaded Bedford Borough Council to install a 'nest-box' scheme in July 1987 and since then the Basel scheme has been adopted by Ely Cathedral in Cambridgeshire, Barking and Dagenham Borough Council and by some railway companies.

Starlings and Sparrows

Both of these common species were once widely regarded as nuisances in many towns and cities. In the 1980s huge flocks of starlings became a tourist attraction in London as congregations of tens of thousands of birds performed amazing aerial manoeuvres before settling in their roosts to the accompaniment of a deafening crescendo of high-pitched chattering. Under such roosts large deposits of droppings accumulated on ledges and pavements. When the roosts were in trees any grass underneath was quickly killed. In London, the City of Westminster used to spend tens of thousands of pounds annually cleaning up after flocks of starlings. Other large cities suffered similar problems. In Toulouse on 21 December 1977, three cyclists, four motorcyclists and a bus skidded on starling droppings. Four people were injured and the bus destroyed a bus shelter. Although bird strikes involving starlings are rare, large flocks roosting near airports can be a danger. The species was responsible for the crash of the Lockheed Electra at Boston, Massachusetts in 1960 with the loss of 62 lives. However, such huge concentrations of starlings are mysteriously no more in the United Kingdom. One day of course, the cycle may turn and the problems may return.

In gardens, starlings may have quite an impact on fruit such as cherries, but traditional scaring tactics such as hanging fluttering metallic ribbons, or ambushing the birds with powerful water-squirting toys, or covering the trees with bird netting will prevent damage reaching unacceptable levels.

Sparrows too have declined dramatically over the last decade or two. When I was a boy in Somerset, the chattering of sparrows perched along our roof guttering was an ever-present noise. In November 1925, a survey of birds in Kensington Gardens recorded that of 3,900 birds, 2,600 were House sparrows. In 1975 sparrow numbers had fallen to around 500. By 1995 only 81 were present while in 2000 only 8 remained.

The latest theory suggested by world expert Denis Summers-Smith night explain why the major decline of sparrows occurred in big cities in the late 1970s and early 1980s. This period coincides with the conversion of leaded to unleaded petrol. Summers-Smith suggests that the chemical methyl tertiary-butyl ether (MTBE) added to unleaded petrol as an 'anti-knocking' agent is killing off small insects that baby sparrows are fed on during the first few days of their life. If true, this may explain why the decline in cities has been more marked than in rural areas.

Nowadays, there are hardly enough House sparrows to justify anyone complaining of them as a nuisance, but occasionally they enter warehouses used to store human or animal food. The amount of food they can take is negligible, but their droppings can represent a health hazard as birds can be infected with salmonellae and other pathogens. House sparrows are still on the list of birds which may be killed or taken at any time of the year by authorised persons, but even the manual produced by the Agricultural Development and Advisory Service (ADAS) and the British Pest Control Association advises:

> 'The house sparrow population in the UK is dramatically declining, and proofing is likely to be regarded as more acceptable than attempts at population control. Where food stores are involved "proofing" should always be considered first.'

Where sparrows have gained access to food warehouses it is possible to trap large numbers of the birds in cage traps. Recommended traps have small wire cones at ground level through which the birds to enter the traps to get at bait such as cake and bread crumbs. Once captured the birds can be released outside the building – hopefully with proofing preventing re-entry.

With a little ingenuity it may be possible to deter sparrows from entering warehouses by hanging cut out shapes of birds of prey such as sparrow hawks in door-ways, or, even using more modern technology such as holograms, regularly flashing an image of such a predator around the inside of the building.

Crows

The corvidae family, magpie, carrion crow, jay, jackdaw, rook and raven are probably the most intelligent of birds. Yet they are traditionally, and irrationally, the most despised and feared of our British bird life. In urban areas crows have become much more noticeable over recent years – provoking many letters to newspaper editors, claiming that the crows have destroyed all our songbirds. Similar unsubstantiated claims are aimed at magpies and it is a sad fact that no matter how much scientific evidence is produced by the RSPB and the British Trust for Ornithology (BTO) to show that magpies have virtually no impact on small bird populations, once a person becomes a magpie hater, in my experience their mind is closed for ever.

Like pigeons, foxes, grey squirrels and rats, carrion crows and magpies flourish in our urban areas because we provide them with larger quantities and a wider variety of food than they could ever find in a wild environment.

When I was a boy growing up in rural Somerset, one of the old country sayings was, 'If you see a rook on its own it's a crow.' This was a way of remembering that rooks nest in colonies in tall trees whereas crows normally occur singly or in pairs. However, the most successful of species are those which adapt to prevailing conditions. Near my home in south-east London, it is quite usual to count around a hundred crows wandering around Winn's Common, part of Plumstead Common. Similar numbers can be seen at any time on nearby Blackheath. I walk my dog on Winn's Common every day and there are at least five people to my certain knowledge who arrive every day, rain or shine, with vast quantities of food for the birds, mostly bread but also fruit, rice and even meat on occasions. To supplement this bonanza, there are still dozens of dog walkers who never clear up their dogs faeces and the crows have no scruples about searching through dog faeces to seek out the undigested bits. Indeed were it not for the crows' provision of this initial breaking-up of the droppings and the consequential faster degradation by insects and the weather, the Common would probably not be fit for the human recreation and sports that take place there all year round!

A few pigeons have also learned what times food deliveries are dropped off at Winn's Common, but they have to be careful not to get surrounded too closely by the crows as on more than one occasion I have seen the crows suddenly mob a pigeon and add it to their diet. A dog-walker acquaintance recently described to me how she managed to intervene in one such attack and rescue a dazed and virtually bald pigeon – for which the People's Dispensary for Sick Animals (PDSA) managed to find a temporary home until its feathers grew again.

None of the crow family can be described as a threat to the well-being of urban dwellers and even in the countryside most of the 'crimes' levelled against them are exaggerated, imaginary or, as is often the case, the fault of humans. True, members of the corvid family can cause a little damage to crops such as cereals and potatoes, but their main persecutors are gamekeepers who object to them taking the odd gamebird egg or chick destined for shooting.

Some sheep farmers destroy crows illegally with poison (that often kills rare and protected birds and animals instead). Their justification for this is that crows peck out the eyes of lambs and sheep. This is certainly true if dead sheep and lambs are left lying out in the open too long, and occasionally may even be suffered by a living lamb or sheep, but only if it has been immobilised by injury or has somehow managed to get cast on its back. Like other forms of predation, such as the rare attack on a lamb by a fox, both DEFRA and the Department of Agriculture and Fisheries for Scotland (DAFS), confirm that healthy and viable lambs and sheep rarely fall victim. It is on the most overstocked farms, and on hill farms where the animals are left out on the bleak hills without supervision, where problems may arise.

In urban areas, complaints about members of the crow family are much more trivial. Some people complain that crows are too 'big' and intimidating. Others think there are 'just too many of them'. I have even had people tell me that they object to crows just sitting in their trees!

There are cases where jackdaws roosting in large numbers on buildings cause damage by contamination and sometimes by blocking chimneys with their nests – this can represent a fire hazard. These nuisances can be combated by installing proofing systems of the same type used to prevent pigeons roosting, and by placing wire screening over chimneys.

Disgracefully, all members of the corvid family, with the exception of the raven, can be killed legally by authorised persons, at any time of the year, including the nesting season. An 'authorised person' is anyone who has the permission of the landowner to carry out the killing. European Bird directives forbid the killing of any birds, even 'pests', during the nesting season for two good reasons. Firstly such killing leaves dependent chicks to slowly starve to death, and secondly, as most killing is with guns, there would be huge disruption and disturbance of non-target birds while nesting. Yet in Britain, our Government has negotiated an 'opt-out' that allows for the slaughter of around a dozen species of birds during the nesting season. The two most glaring examples of this are, firstly, the shooting with shotguns of rooks every July while the birds are roosting in their rookeries and, secondly, the use of captured magpies, kept confined in cage traps and used as decoys to attract other magpies into another compartment of the trap. These traps, widely used by gamekeepers, and known as Larsen traps after their Scandinavian inventor, are responsible for the deaths of tens of thousands of magpies every year. Under European directives it is illegal to capture wild birds and keep them in cages, but once again Britain has an opt-out from such laws in respect of corvids.

Whatever the arguments for using lethal methods in the countryside, there is certainly no justification for such extreme measures in urban areas. For those who insist that the corvid family are responsible for the decline in other bird species, and particularly songbirds, consider the evidence from my area of Plumstead in urban southeast London. Mark Angliss, a member of the Plumstead

Common Environment Group, studied the wildlife on and around the Common. He described crows, magpies and jays as 'abundant', but his record of sightings between July and October 1999, would make any ornithologist envious. They were: Cormorant, Grey heron, Canada goose, Mallard, Sparrowhawk, Kestrel, Moorhen, Black-headed gull, Herring gull, Great blackbacked gull, Lesser black-backed gull, Feral pigeon, Woodpigeon, Collared dove, Swift, Green woodpecker, Great-spotted wood-pecker, Robin, Skylark, Swallow, House martin, Meadow pipit, Pied wagtail, Grey wagtail, Dunnock, Sedge warbler, Whitethroat, Blackcap, Chiffchaff, Goldcrest, Spotted flycatcher, Wheatear, Blackbird, Song thrush, Mistle thrush, Fieldfare, Longtailed tit, Great tit, Blue tit, Wren, Greenfinch, Goldfinch, House sparrow and Starling.

Gulls

Herring and Lesser black-backed gulls, like pigeons and most species of corvids, as well as starlings and sparrows, can be legally taken or killed by authorised persons at any time of the year. On the other hand, Black-headed and Common gulls are protected. Complaints about Herring and Black-backed gulls are increasing annually, most concerning damaged roofs, nests on chimneys and gutters blocked with nest debris. There are also complaints of gulls fouling buildings and washing on lines, making excessive noise and mobbing people for food.

Concern has also been raised about gulls feeding on refuse tips and carrying rubbish such as cans and polythene bags to resting areas such as nearby fields, thus introducing a hazard to grazing animals. It is also possible for gulls to pollute reservoirs and streams with salmonella that originates from refuse tips.

Proper management of refuse tips reduces such risks. On landfill sites care needs to be taken to ensure that rubbish is quickly covered with soil to a depth beyond the beaks of powerful birds. Frequent disturbance, netting or even scarers such as the Helikite balloon that simulates a hovering bird of prey, are all methods of reducing problems at rubbish tips.

The problems of gulls damaging roofs and nesting on chimneys can be countered by proofing. A recent innovation, Gullguard, is designed specifically to deter seagulls from urban areas. It consists of a set of plastic base units supporting 3 mm stainless steel wires which form a raised 'net' 20 cm above the area to be protected. The inventors have calculated that most gulls stand upright with their body 12–18 cm above the structure upon which they are standing and have a wing span of around 1.5 m. Unlike some birds, pigeons for instance, gulls need a short run to take off in still conditions. Gullguard, obtainable from Killgerm, simply restricts the gull's wing span and take-off run. The modular system is flexible enough to make different configurations and placing this device on roofs is a permanent way of keeping gulls from landing, resting and taking off, thus forcing them to seek more comfortable locations.

Some seaside town local authorities have responded to complaints from residents by resorting to lethal control methods, and a huge controversy erupted in Edinburgh in the year 2000 when the local council announced a decision to start killing seagulls. The protests by bird lovers and animal rights groups were so vociferous that the council postponed the plan and set up a Seagull Focus Group to reconsider the issue. On 30 November 2000 the council's Chief Environmental Health Officer reported that after wide consultation it had been decided to implement alternative action consisting of public education about feeding, the provision of birdproof litter bins and refuse sacks, the proofing of Council owned property where gulls were nesting and roosting, and to consider control measures at landfill sites. It was also decided to monitor the number of gulls and nests in Dumfries on an annual basis.

Clearly a case of public protest resulting in the adoption of Council policies based on common sense!

Canada Geese

The Canada goose was first introduced to Britain in the late seventeenth century as an ornamental attraction for the gardens and parks of the aristocracy. However the population explosion of the birds only really started in the 1970s, when the population was estimated at only 19,000 birds. Today there are more than 60,000, in part due to increase in lakes formed by disused gravel pits. The geese favour lowland waters and they tend to return every year to breed where they were born and reared. They breed from the age of two or three years and their clutches vary from 3 to 11 eggs laid in April. Incubation by the female lasts for a month.

Complaints about Canada geese vary greatly. Farmers complain that large flocks of the geese damage growing crops and pasture, but in urban areas the main allegation is the fouling of parks, gardens, footpaths and lake edges. Clearly such sizeable birds congregating in large flocks and defecating every few minutes, produce a lot of unpleasant excreta. Tabloid newspapers can be relied upon to publish as many scare stories about Canada geese as they do about pigeons and rats. The media regularly denigrates them using words such as 'noisy and aggressive', 'aliens', 'health hazards' and other pejorative phrases. One newspaper made allegations, but offered no actual evidence, of humans being infected with diarrhoea or gastro-enteritis from picnicking in parks grazed by Canada geese, or from handling golf balls contaminated by Canada geese droppings on golf courses, or of native wildfowl suffering population declines due to the presence of the 'alien'.

This attitude has led to clandestine culls of the birds in some of London's parks and, inevitably, the formation of Canada geese defence groups. Legally, as with many other species of goose and duck, Canada geese can be legally shot by authorised persons on land from 1 September to 31 January (or 1 September to 20 February below high-water mark). Outside these periods killing or taking of the birds or their eggs is an offence unless a licence has been obtained either from DEFRA or from the equivalent Welsh or Scottish environment department.

Officially licences can be granted only for the following purposes:

- to conserve wild birds;
- to protect any collection of wild birds;
- to preserve public heath or public or air safety;
- to prevent serious damage to livestock, foodstuffs for livestock, crops, vegetables, fruit, growing timber or fisheries.

The Wildlife & Countryside Act 1981 does not allow licences to be issued if the only purpose of the killing is to prevent damage to property including amenity land However, licences have been issued for the killing of Canada geese in public parks, ostensibly on the grounds that the geese are either threatening public safety through their excreta or are threatening other wild birds. Although there are claims that Canada geese are aggressive to other wildfowl, I witnessed two large Canada geese being driven off a small floating island on a pond on Plumstead Common by a tiny Moorhen that had chosen the island for its nest site!

Each application for a licence to take or kill Canada Geese must, in theory at least, justify the reasons for which a licence is required and must also show that other non-lethal methods of control, such as scaring, either are not applicable or have failed. But it is doubtful whether much serious investigation has been conducted into finding alternatives to killing adult geese and destroying eggs.

In the birds' native Canada there is evidence of a more

intelligent approach. In the summer of the year 2000 my wife and I visited Calgary, where we learned that in the previous summer, paths through the city's new Prince's Park were often dangerously slippery due to large quantities of excreta deposited by native Canada geese. And yet on our visit one year later there was not a Canada goose to be seen and the paths and grass were completely clear of bird droppings. We made enquiries and found that the park authority had solved the problem without harming a single Goose and without even breaking an egg – simply by applying knowledge of the species and a little logic.

The first step in the authority's campaign was to place notices throughout the park in an effort to persuade the public not to encourage the birds with food. However, using an imaginative tactic that British local authorities would do well to adopt, instead of merely threatening people with fines for feeding birds, the Canadians appealed to the consciences of the bird feeders with notices to the effect that: 'How healthy would you be living on a diet of bread? and 'Feed 'em in the summer and you'll starve 'em in the winter'.

The next stage was to employ people to study the birds during the breeding season and to watch where the birds were nesting. When the eggs appeared they were collected and placed in incubators. When the goslings hatched they were transported to a lake some distance from the city where they were promptly adopted by the Canada geese resident on the lake. The goslings became imprinted with that lake as their natal habitat. Back in the city park, wardens awaited the July summer moult of the adult's flight feathers so that when the birds could not escape, they were rounded up, loaded into air-conditioned trucks and transported out of town to the lake to be re-united with their offspring. The result? Complete success!

Of course Canada is the true home of the geese, and in an overcrowded British countryside landowners might not welcome flocks of city geese and goslings being dumped upon their lakes. But where Canada geese are causing sufficient problems to warrant applications for licences for destruction, their capture and removal to suitable lakes should at least be considered. Under the Wildlife & Countryside Act 1981, Canada geese are amongst those alien wild birds and animals that cannot be legally released in the United Kingdom, so a special licence would be required if the Calgary scheme was adopted. If such a scheme is rejected, the destruction of eggs, disturbance of nest sites and discouragement of feeding should all be vital parts of long-term and logical programmes of control, rather than shooting the existing adults. And we need much more research and knowledge before we blindly accept claims that Canada geese, being large foreign birds, are causing problems for our native species of wildfowl.

B. SMALL

Herons

Ponds containing fish and amphibians will sooner or later be visited by a heron – and if the bird successfully obtains a meal it will return time and time again. Nets are available to keep herons from ponds, but may spoil the aesthetic value of the pond. The nets need to be kept taut at least 75 cm above the water and the mesh size needs to be smaller than 5 cm to prevent a heron thrusting its neck through.

Another option for the protection of ponds from birds as well as deterring cats or foxes from hunting fish or frogs, is the Scarecrow. This device is battery powered and consists basically of an infrared PIR detector and a sprinkler head. When a standard garden hose pipe is fitted to the device and the battery switched on, any bird or animal that approaches within 10 metres, is scared off by a sudden 3-second burst of water from the sprinkler head. Considering that the fish in a pond may be Coy Carp worth hundreds of pounds each, then the Scarecrow is a worthwhile investment – its only drawbacks being that it cannot be used during very frosty weather and that it needs to be sited so that it is not being repeatedly triggered by the movement of shrubs in the wind.

The Royal Society for the Protection of Birds (RSPB) has produced a helpful leaflet on protecting ponds from herons and recommends the erection of a 2-strand fence at the very edge of the pond. Herons like to land a little distance from the water and walk to the bank. A fence will prevent this, but if it is erected too far from the edge, the heron will merely land inside the fence. The strands should be of polypropylene twine and its effect may be enhanced by tying fluttering ribbons to it.

The RSPB also recommends placing shrubs near the pond as herons are nervous of being ambushed and prefer to fish where they can see any danger coming. Yet another solution is to place a chain of polythylene floats around the margin of the pool, spaced less than 30 cm apart. Herons don't like fishing between or over the floats.

Many people have tried placing plastic herons at the pond side on the principle that herons flying over will be wary of encroaching on another heron's feeding station. However, in practice the plastic heron is more likely to attract other herons than deter them.

Feeding Birds

The history of pigeon control shows that the popular pastime of feeding pigeons and other birds in squares and parks, or of ducks at the local pond or even of blackbirds and bluetits in our gardens, needs careful thinking through – as it does for any wild creatures.

For instance, if you erect a bird table in the garden, or hang a bird feeder from the clothes line, not only will you get the birds you like, but you will also attract predators such as sparrow hawks and cats. If you do not keep the bird table scrupulously clean by scrubbing it at least every week with a safe disinfectant it could rapidly become a source of bacteria and diseases such as botulism that will kill the birds you intended to thrive!

Food knocked off the table by the birds will attract rats, and urban foxes will visit nightly to see if there is a snack worth scavenging. Personally, I think it is safer to grow plants that bear fruit, seeds and berries and leave the rest to nature, rather than providing either unnatural foods or natural foods at unnatural times of the year.

As for dealing with nuisance birds, the same principles apply as with nuisance mammals. If you don't want them, don't provide them with the food or shelter they need. If you have such attractions and want to keep them, then you must either prevent the unwelcome creatures from getting to them, or use repellents or other deterrents to keep them away.

Simulated Predators and Other Tactics

A recent simple innovation designed to deter birds by simulating their predator, consists of a helium balloon fixed to a kite. Suitable for the protection of commercial ventures such as farms, orchards, landfill sites, fish farms, office blocks, sports centres and hotels, the Helikite is tethered to the ground and hovers like a large bird of prey at heights of up to 60 metres. Birds such as pigeons, rooks, starlings and finches have been preyed upon throughout their evolution by birds of prey, and a flying object hovering high in the sky above them is enough to persuade them to move out of the hawk's range. The 'hawk' is produced by Allsopp Helikites.

Such a device is not really suitable for protecting small gardens, where flapping tin foil, nets, the Scarecrow mentioned earlier, and other simple scaring tactics are normally more than adequate.

A problem sometimes arises when a roosting site chosen by birds results in their droppings damaging cars parked below, or on paths, rendering them slippery and dangerous. Urban wood pigeons in particular like to roost in some of the large leafy sycamore trees that line many roads in suburbia. If the roost is near enough to an upper-floor window, it may be possible (taking the utmost care over personal safety, of course) to drive the birds off by squirting them with water using a children's water gun. Many large toyshops carry a range of powerful toy water squirters ranging in price (at the time of writing) from around £15 to £40. If the tree can be climbed safely, tying strips of flapping plastic or metallic ribbon to the twigs and branches used by the birds, may be enough to persuade them either to abandon the tree altogether or at least to move the roost to another part of the tree. Failing that the services of a tree surgeon could be employed to remove the actual branches used by the birds. If the tree is growing on land, such as the roadside, owned by the local authority, you may be able to persuade the council to employ its own staff or contractors to carry out the work.

The Future

The Future

The purpose of this book is to save lives and prevent the suffering of animals and birds that may occasionally cause us problems in urban areas. I hope that readers experiencing annoyance or damage because a wild creature is sharing their habitat will firstly try to be a little tolerant and accept that it's nothing personal. Secondly, I hope that people who have a genuine problem with wild animals or birds will try some of the tactics described in the pages of this book or will seek advice from a knowledgeable person or group motivated by compassion rather than profit. A conventional pest control company should be a last resort and then, only one of those that have a reputation for professionalism. There are as many 'cowboys' in the world of pest control as there are in other professions. If in doubt check credentials with the British Pest Control Association (BPCA).

Pest control is a £multi-billion industry which deals out suffering and death to millions of living creatures not only in the developed world but, increasingly, the third world also. Highly toxic products such as the parasiticide DDT (dicholorodiphenyl-trychlorethane) and the insecticides Dieldrin and BHC (benzene hexachloride) have been responsible for much misery, as have poisons such as the anti-coagulant Warfarin (for poisoning rats, mice and squirrels) and strychnine (for poisoning moles) – both of which poisons have killed countless numbers of non-target animals through secondary poisoning or deliberate misuse. Many businesses, factories, warehouses and food outlets have contracts with pest control companies whose operatives turn up regularly to place poison bait in plastic hoppers distributed around the premises. No one seems to realise that regularly placing such bait around buildings is bound to attract rodent scavengers which otherwise might not be there!

Spring traps, guns, gas and poisons are just four methods of killing nuisance creatures, but surely the perfect example of man's wicked deviousness is the use of 'sticky-boards' for capturing rats and mice. These rodent boards consist of sheets of hardboard or plastic coated with glue. The rodents walk across the boards and become totally stuck to the surface until removed and killed – sometimes many hours later. The fear and distress of such trapped animals can only be imagined.

We humans display a strange attitude to wildlife. If the animal is a member of a rare species it becomes protected by law. With endangered species we pass laws that not only protect the creature from deliberate persecution, but also impose severe penalties for merely disturbing the animal. We have even employed the British army to defend the nests of rare birds of prey such as Peregrine falcons.

Yet beware any animal with a biology that enables it to thrive. If the animal or bird is not rare enough to figure in the lists of protected species, then people are free to kill as many as they like merely for amusement. Thus people with guns, not content with shooting at non-sentient targets, slaughter millions of living, feeling birds without a qualm. Worse, in order to preserve sufficient living targets to be killed, these people employ other people to kill other wild creatures that might, in order to survive, eat one of their 'targets'.

If our conservation efforts succeed and the previously rare animal species recovers to become numerous, our concern for their death and suffering is suddenly forgotten – until of course they become rare again. For the life of me I have never been able to understand why an animal which is of a rare species should be protected from cruelty, persecution and slaughter, while any creature fortunate enough to thrive in reasonable numbers can be tortured for amusement and killed at any time by almost any method. It is remarkable that until the Wild Mammals (Protection) Act 1996, piloted through Parliament by Labour Member of Parliament Alan Meale (whom I had the honour of assisting during the passage of his Bill), wild mammals in Britain, with only few exceptions, could be beaten, kicked, stabbed, drowned, impaled and even burnt without transgressing any laws.

And as I write these words, people are still free to use dogs to hound deer, foxes, hares, mink and other wild animals to exhaustion and death in the name of entertainment. It is also permissible to set wire snares to capture, maim and strangle countless thousands of foxes and rabbits despite the fact that many non-target and so-called protected species become accidental casualties in these appalling traps.

A glaring example of our illogical attitude to wildlife is our different attitudes to wild animals and wild birds. The principle of wild bird protection is that they, their eggs, their young and their nests are all protected from persecution – apart from those that are listed as exceptions. However, the principle of wild mammal protection is the complete opposite; none of them are protected from persecution, apart from those on a list of exceptions! Why should this be?

It is high time that as a nation we evolved a 'wildlife management department' of government, and in principle protected *all* wild mammals and birds. Then we can argue what creatures need to be exceptions and what tactics and weaponry can be used and by whom. If we had a wildlife management department headed by a Minister or at least as part of the Department of the Environment, Food and Rural Affairs, it would be accountable to the electorate. Where wildlife causes a problem to farming, forestry, or any other industry, sports club, or even individuals, advice could be sought from the Wildlife Management Department's nearest regional office. That office would be responsible for conducting research, keeping abreast of techniques evolving in other countries, providing up-to-date advice on permissible methods of dealing with problems, and if necessary providing grants for fences and other defences. The department could also provide professional and accountable experts trained in techniques including the skills of marksmanship in the event of culls being considered necessary.

The point is, wildlife belongs either to no one or to everyone. We have already adopted the principle of the state being responsible for the protection of rare and endangered species, in the same way that the state has the power to intervene where people are found to be inflicting cruelty onto their own animals. In 1996 the nation, through Parliament, adopted the power to intervene in cases of certain acts of cruelty to wild mammals. There is no reason why this power should not be extended to all cover forms of unnecessary suffering and unnecessary killing of wild mammals.

A government Department of Wildlife Management would be accessible to all sectors of the community and would ensure that the fate of wildlife in Britain was not, as it is now, in the hands of landowners and those they choose to allow on their land. Farmers complaining that deer are damaging crops or overgrazing pasture needed for domestic livestock could contact their local Department office where accountable staff could investigate and if necessary develop a plan to resolve the problem. It may involve a grant for fencing, or compensation for damage, or even sending in trained marksmen to carry out a properly calculated cull. Local wildlife conservation bodies and animal welfare interests would be free to contribute their ideas and opinions, but in the end the decision would be made by professionals. Surely this would be much better than local deer hunters charging into the area for the fun of hounding deer around the local community, through gardens, into village centres, and over main roads and railways, or the job being left to shooting enthusiasts who are accountable to no one if they bodge the operation or inflict unnecessary suffering.

In urban areas, existing 'pest' control companies would be accountable to, and sub-contracted by, the local Wildlife Management Department. This should eliminate the cowboy element. I have heard of one so-called pest control company operating in the South East of England that uses terrier dogs to drive fox cubs into nets (for a fat fee), telling the client that the cubs will be released in a 'fox sanctuary'. In fact in some cases this firm has taken the cubs to a local voluntary wildlife rescue centre, dumped them on the counter saying: 'You take them, or we kill them' – which of course leaves the wildlife centre staff without any choice. There are other pest controllers who admit to trapping foxes and dumping them in other areas. They clearly don't advise their clients that removal of the foxes will merely create a vacancy for other foxes to fill or that the foxes they have dumped will have great difficulty surviving in a strange territory vigorously defended by other foxes!

A state Wildlife Management Department on the other hand would have education as a major role and could distribute a wide range of leaflets based on the latest scientific evidence rather than the ignorance, mythology and superstition spread around by those with dubious motives for promoting the killing of wildlife.

At the moment, the science of combating wildlife nuisance with non-lethal deterrence tactics is very much in its infancy. But it is growing as more people demand methods that satisfy their consciences. One day, we may see fleets of vehicles bearing names such as Sendemoff or Repell'em. But meanwhile, I would like to hear from any technological wizards, lateral thinkers, naturalists and wildlife behaviourists who have ideas for non-harmful resolutions of conflicts between man and animal and who can help advance this revolution.

Appendix 1
Suppliers and Manufacturers of Repellents and Deterrents

Electranets Ltd (electric fencing)
31 Westfield Avenue
Brockworth
Gloucester
GL3 4AU
Tel: 01452 864230
Fax: 01452 617841
e-mail: em.Roy@electranets.fsnet.co.uk

Get Off My Garden & Wash and Get Off
Pet and Garden Manufacturing plc
The Old Creamery
Queens Road
Sanquhar
Dumfries
Scotland
DG4 6DN
Tel: 01659 50141
Fax: 01659 50142
www.pet-and-garden,com

Gullguard (Seagull deterrent)
Killgerm Chemicals Limited
PO Box 2
Ossett
West Yorkshire
WF5 9NA
Tel: 01924 268400
Fax: 01924 264757
e-mail: sales@killgerm.com
www.killgerm.com

Helikite (bird scarer)
Allsopp Helikites Ltd
South End Farm
Damerham
Fordingbridge
Hampshire
SP6 3HW
Tel: 01725 518750
Fax: 01725 518786
e-mail: allsopp@helikites.com
www.helikites.com

Humane (live capture) mole, rat, rabbit and squirrel cage traps, pond covers and garden repellents
Agriframes Ltd
Charlwoods Road
East Grinstead
West Sussex
RH19 2HP
Tel: 01342 310000
e-mail: sales@agriframes.co.uk
www.agriframes.co.uk

Pigeon deterrents

Flock-Off (UK) Limited,
PO Box 92,
Ware,
Herts
SG11 2BD
Tel: 01279 503250
Fax: 01279 659133
e-mail: eppltd@indigo.ie
www.indigo.ie/eppltd

Deben Netting & Pest Control,
Gore Cross Business Park,
Bradpole,
Bridport,
Dorset
DT6 3UX
Tel: 01308 423576
Fax: 01308 425912
e-mail: npc@deben.com
www.deben.com

Network Pest Control Systems Ltd,
1030 Centre Park
Slutchers Lane
Warrington
Cheshire
WA1 1QR
Tel: 01925 411823
Fax: 01925 414994

Renardine
> Roebuck Eyot,
> 7a Hatfield Way,
> South Church Enterprise Park,
> Bishop Auckland,
> County Durham
> DL14 6XF
> Tel: 01388 772233
> Fax: 01388 775233
> e-mail: sales@roebuck-eyot.co.uk

Scarecrow (water jet)
> Aquatics Online
> 12 The Triangle,
> Brackla
> Bridgend
> CF31 2LL
> Tel: 01656 651149
> Fax: 01656 663427
> E-mail: mail@aquatics-online.co.uk
> www.aquatics-online.co.uk

> East Horticulture
> Rosedale Nursery
> College Road
> Hextable
> Kent
> BR8 7LT
> Tel: 01322 662130
> Fax: 01322 666037
> E-mail: easthort@dircon.co.uk
> www.east-horticulture.co.uk

[In case of any difficulty finding a local outlet, contact the UK distributor – Drivall Ltd, Tel: 0121 423 1122]

Scoot
  William Sinclair Horticulture Ltd,
  Firth Road,
  Lincoln
  LN6 7AH
  Tel: 01522 537561
  Fax: 01522 513209
  info@william-sinclair.co.uk
  www.william-sinclair.co.uk

Sentinel rabbit fencing
  Tinsley Wire Products,
  PO Box 119,
  Shepcote Lane,
  Sheffield,
  S9 1TY
  Tel: 0114 256 1561

Sonic mole chaser (and other ultrasonic devices)
  PestContro
  Tel: 0870 2410147

Ultrasonic Animal Chaser
  Tensor Marketing Ltd,
  Yarm Road Industrial Estate,
  Darlington,
  County Durham
  DL1 4XX
  Tel: 01325 469181
  Fax: 01325 381386
  TensorLtd@aol.com

Appendix 2
Useful Addresses

ADAS (Agriculture, Development and Advisory Service)
Oxford Spires Business Park,
The Boulevard,
Kidlington,
OX15 1NZ
Tel: 01865 842742

British Pest Control Association (BPCA)
Ground Floor
Gleneagles House
Vernongate
Derby
DE1 1UP
Tel: 01322 294288
Fax: 01332 295904
e-mail: enquiry@bcpa.org.uk

Department of the Environment, Food and Rural Affairs (DEFRA)
17 Smith Square
London
SW1P 3JR
Tel: 020 7238 3000

DEFRA (Wildlife Section)
Tollgate House
Houlton Street
Bristol BS2 9DJ
Tel: 0117 987 8000

DEFRA Hotline for reporting suspected poisoning incidents
0800 321600

Humane Urban Wildlife Deterrence
e-mail: enquiries@jbryant.co.uk
www.jbryant.co.uk

Pesticides Safety Directorate
Mallard House
Kings Pool
3 Peasholme Green
York
YO1 7PX
Tel: 01904 640500

Royal Society for the Prevention of Cruelty to Animals (Wildlife Department)
Wilberforce Way
Southwater
Horsham
West Sussex
RH13 9RS
Tel: 0870 0101181
Emergency tel: 0990 555999.

Scottish Office
Agriculture, Environment and Fisheries Department
Pentland House
47 Robb's Loan
Edinburgh
EH14 1TW
Tel: 0131 5567 8400

Scottish Natural Heritage (SNH)
12 Hope Terrace
Edinburgh
EH9 2AS
Tel: 0131 447 4784
Fax: 0131 446 2277

Welsh Office Agriculture Department (WOAD)
Cathays Park
Crown Buildings
Cardiff
CF1 3NQ
Tel: 01222 823555
Fax: 01222 823204

FOXES

The Fox Project
The Old Chapel
Bradford Street
Tonbridge
Kent
TN9 1AW
Tel: 01732 367397
e-mail: vulpes@foxproject.freeserve.co.uk
New web site under construction

Deterrence advice line 0906 2724411 (25p per minute)
Mange advice line 0906 2724422 (25p per minute)

The National Fox Welfare Society
135 Higham Road
Rushden
Northants
NN10 6DS
Tel: 01933 411996
Fax: 01933 397324
e-mail: info@nfws.org.uk
www.nfws.org.uk

SQUIRRELS

Animal Answers Advice line
Tel: 0906 272 4477

BADGERS

National Federation of Badger Groups (NFBG)
Unit 15,
Cloisters House,
Cloisters Business Centre,
8 Battersea Park Road,
London
SW8 4BG
Tel: 020 7498 3220
Fax: 020 7627 4212
e-mail: enquiries@nfbg.org.uk
www.badgers.org.uk/nfbg

Local Badger Protection Group
Details can be obtained from libraries or from the NFBG.

Animal Answers Badger Advice Lines
Feeding and encouragement
    0906 272 4455 (25p per minute)
Legal restrictions for builders/developers
    0906 272 4456 (25p per minute)

BATS

The Bat Conservation Trust
15 Cloisters House
8 Battersea Park Road
London
SW8 4BG
Tel: 020 7627 2629
Fax: 020 7627 2628
E-mail: enquiries@bats.org.uk
www.bats.org.uk

BIRDS

PICAS (Pigeon Control Advisory Service)
29 Victoria Green
Witchford
Cambridgeshire
CB6 2XB
Tel: 01353 667230
E mail: enquiries@picas.org
www.picas.org

Royal Society for the Protection of Birds
The Lodge
Sandy
Bedfordshire
SG19 2DL
Tel: 01767 680551
www.rspb.org.uk

Also by John Bryant:

Animal Sanctuary

Animal Sanctuary is a passionate and humane book about how animals behave if they are treated with decency and respect. John Bryant introduces us to many of the animals he encountered while manager of the Ferne Animal Sanctuary, and shows us how enormously the natural life of these animals differs from the life they experience in conventional farms or when they have to work for a living. Under his pen, the animals become characters with their own personalities; and this gives the book its own special charm. *Animal Sanctuary* will be enjoyed by animal lovers everywhere, pointing, as it does, the way to a more humane future.

ISBN 0 900001 43 7 £6.99